THE
METAMORPHOSIS

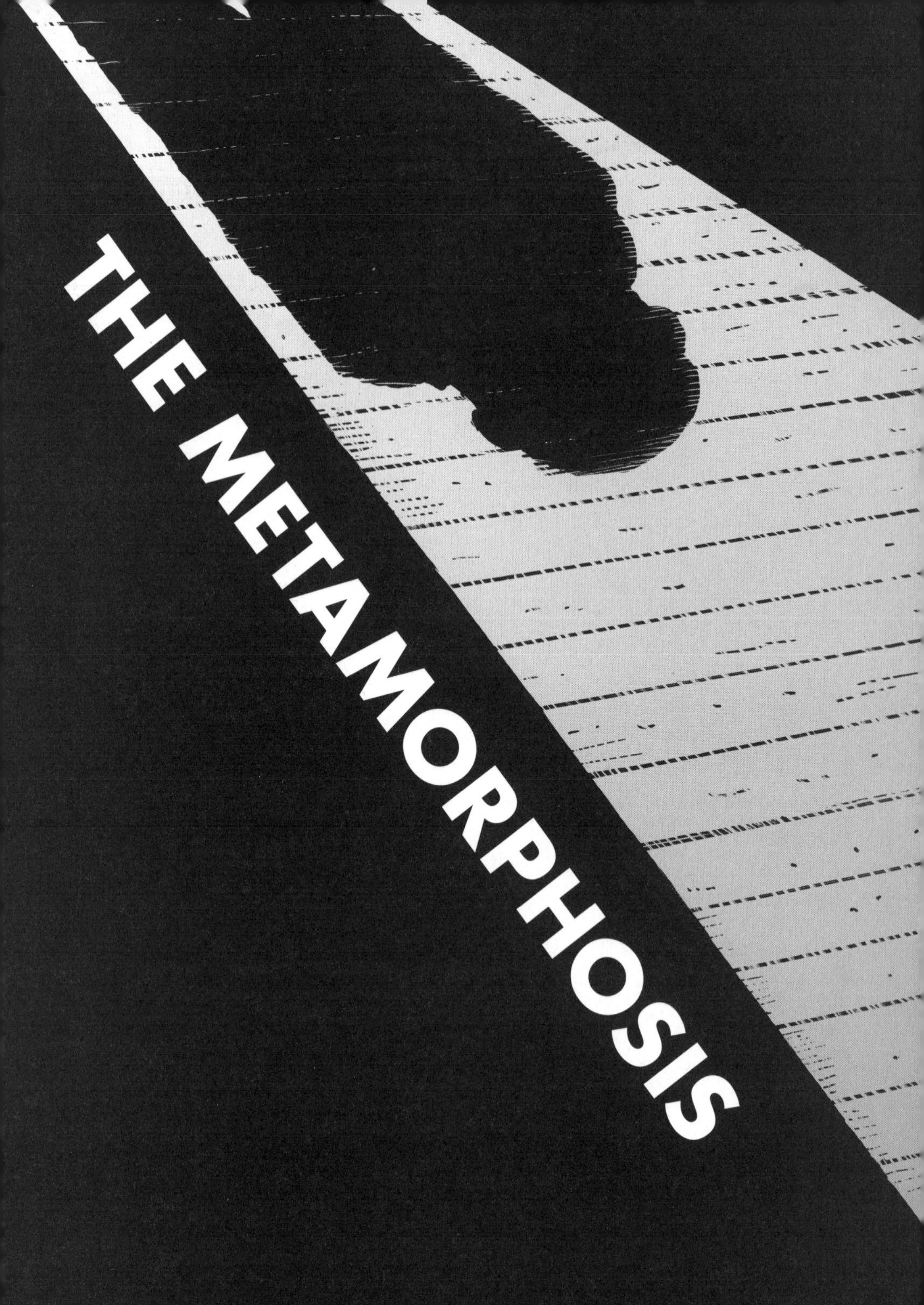

THE METAMORPHOSIS

FRANZ KAFKA

ADAPTED BY **PETER KUPER**

THREE RIVERS PRESS • NEW YORK

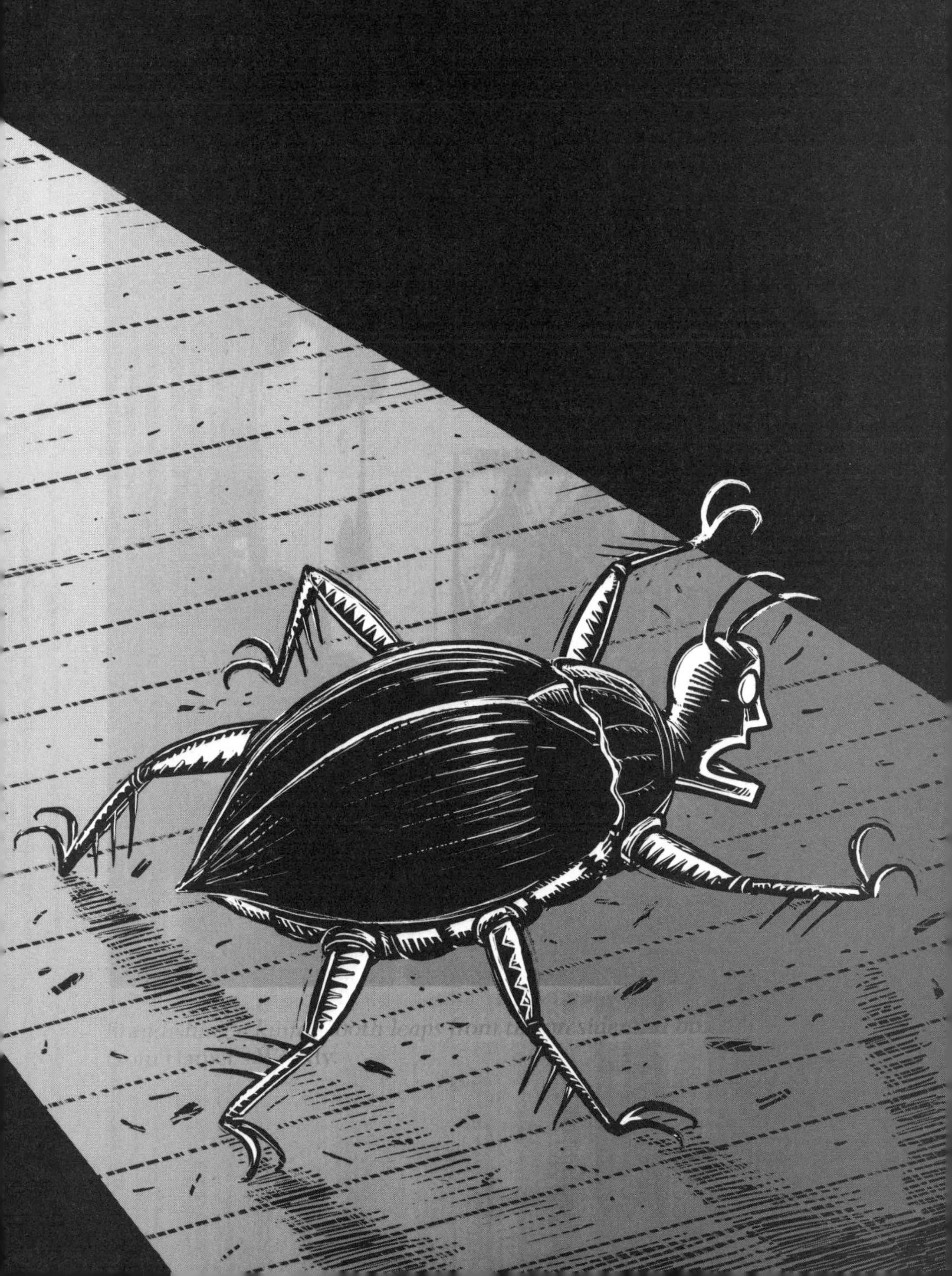

Dedicated to Gregor Samsas everywhere

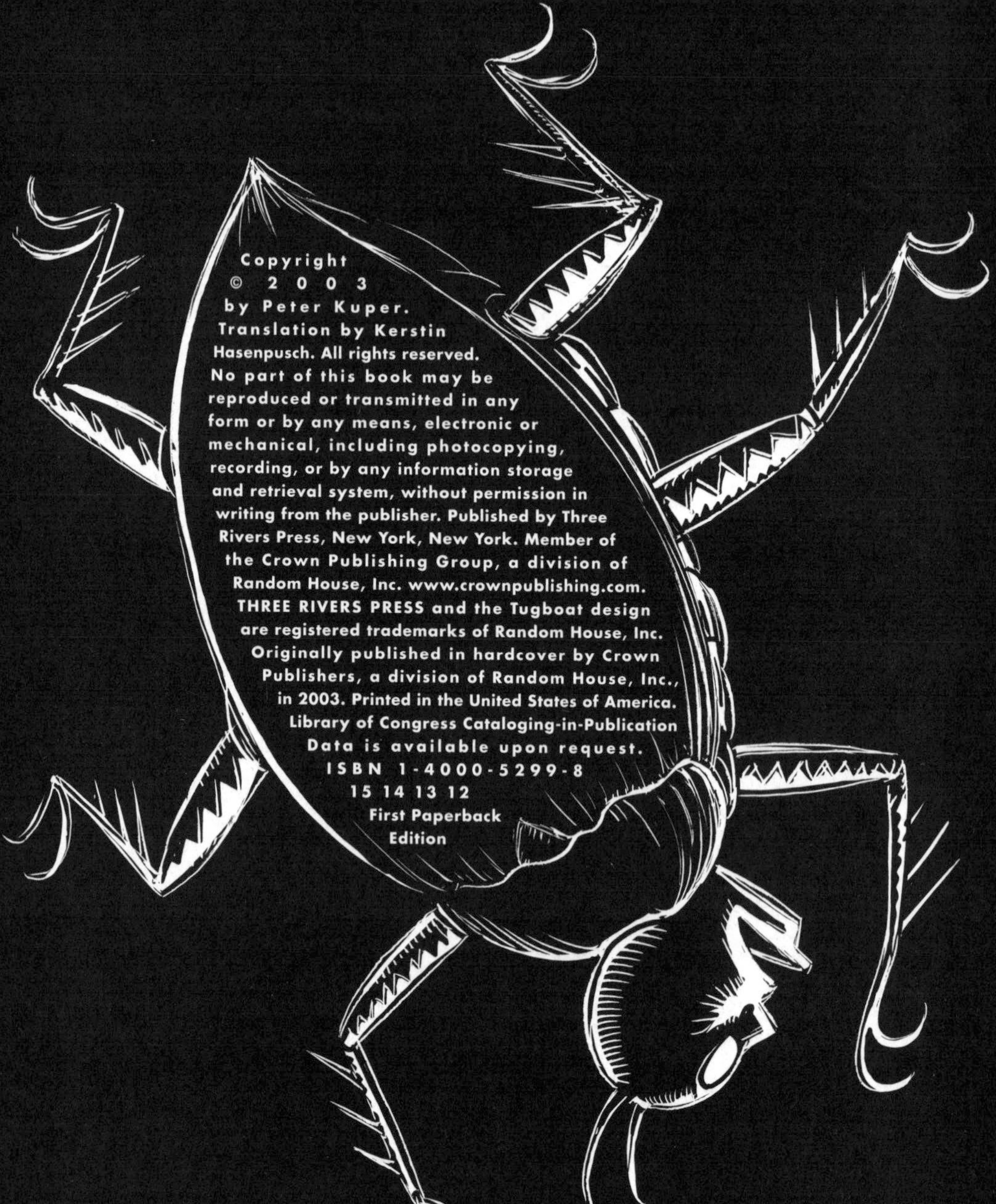

Translation by Kerstin Hasenpusch.

Published by Three Rivers Press, New York, New York. Member of the Crown Publishing Group, a division of Random House, Inc. www.crownpublishing.com.
THREE RIVERS PRESS and the Tugboat design are registered trademarks of Random House, Inc.
Originally published in hardcover by Crown Publishers, a division of Random House, Inc., in 2003. Printed in the United States of America.
Library of Congress Cataloging-in-Publication Data is available upon request.
ISBN 1-4000-5299-8
15 14 13 12
First Paperback Edition

THE INTRODUCTION

In 1904, eight years before Franz Kafka wrote *The Metamorphosis* in Prague, across the ocean a cartoonist named Winsor McCay created "Dream of the Rarebit Fiend," a comic strip that appeared in New York's *Evening Telegram*. In each one-page installment a character was trapped in a world that grew more surreal with each panel—a gentleman's leg inflates and demolishes a mansion, a suitor's lover crumbles into confetti and blows away, a lady's alligator handbag morphs into a monster and devours her. Finally, in the last panel, the character awakens to reality, vowing never again to eat the nightmare-inducing rarebit cheese before bedtime.

Of course, Franz Kafka never allowed his characters to enjoy the relief of awakening to normalcy from their disturbing dreams. Still, the two artists had much in common, including a shared genius for rendering the anxious intersection of reality and dreamscape. Kafka may never have been a comic strip fan, but his angst-ridden characters in reality-bending scenarios are ideally suited to this medium. This adaptation of *The Metamorphosis* couldn't exist without Kafka's illuminating words, but owes a visual debt to McCay's trailblazing excursions into the absurd darkness of slumberland. I have drawn tremendous inspiration from both these pioneers, fascinated by their ability to address our human condition with unexpected twists, brilliant artistry, and deadpan humor.

Nearly a century later, the works of Kafka and McCay seem as fresh as if they were created to reflect our current zeitgeist. Kafka's tales of nightmare trials and monolithic bureaucracies feel no more surreal than headlines from our daily newspapers. It makes one wish that simply avoiding rarebit cheese were the remedy.

—Peter Kuper

When Gregor Samsa
awoke one morning from
disturbing dreams,
he found himself
transformed . . .

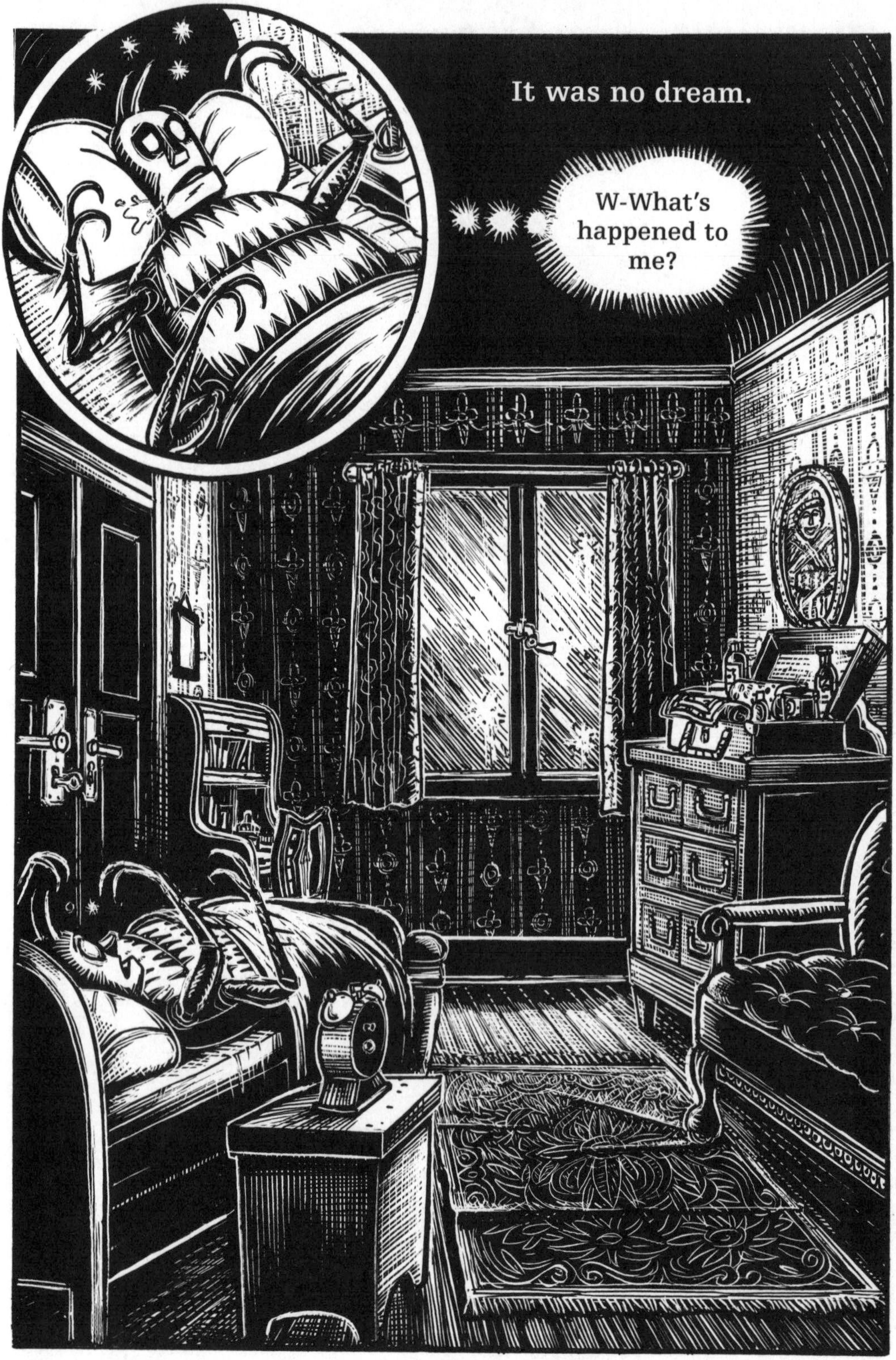
It was no dream.
W-What's happened to me?

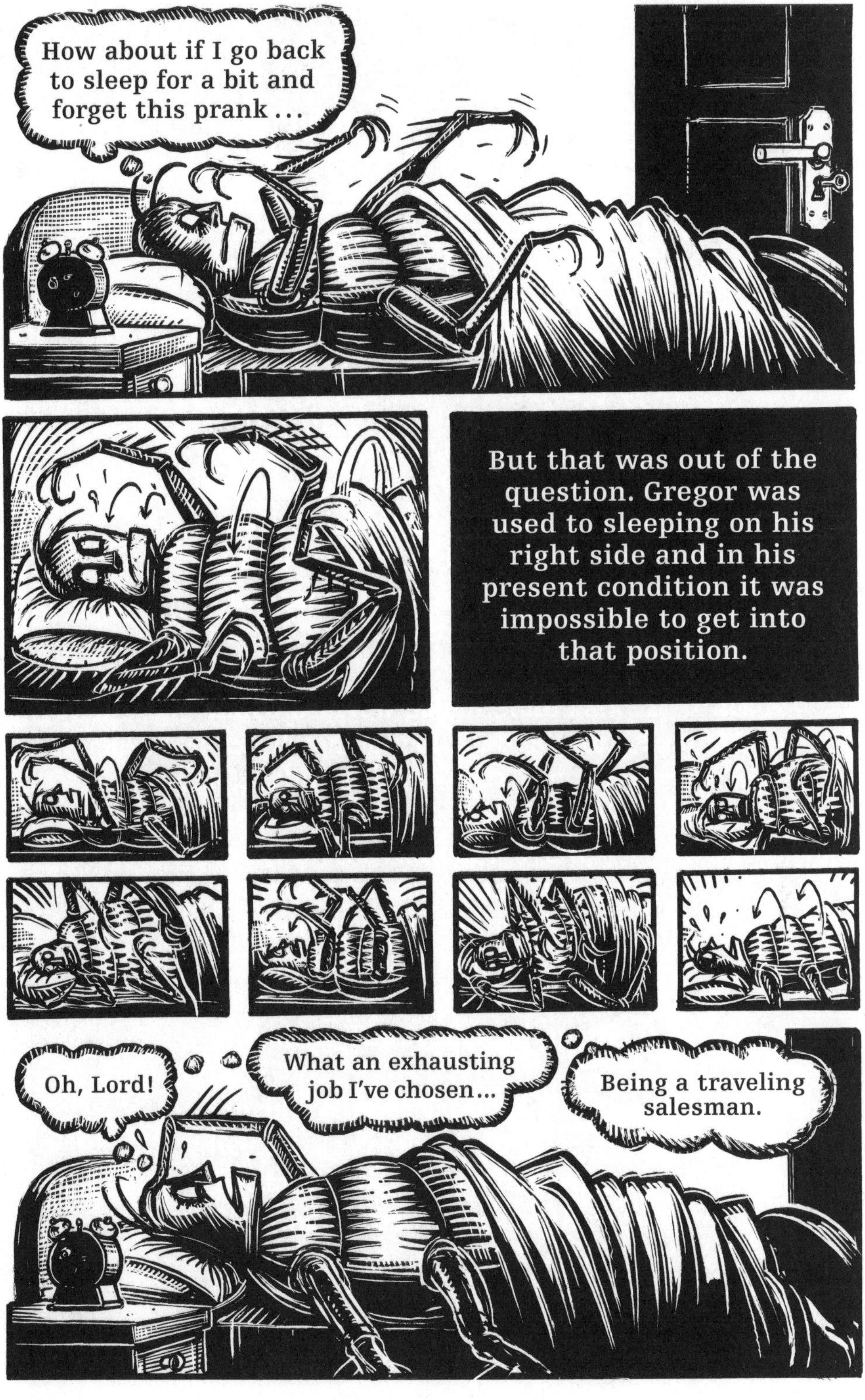
How about if I go back to sleep for a bit and forget this prank . . .
But that was out of the question. Gregor was used to sleeping on his right side and in his present condition it was impossible to get into that position.
Oh, Lord!
What an exhausting job I've chosen...
Being a traveling salesman.

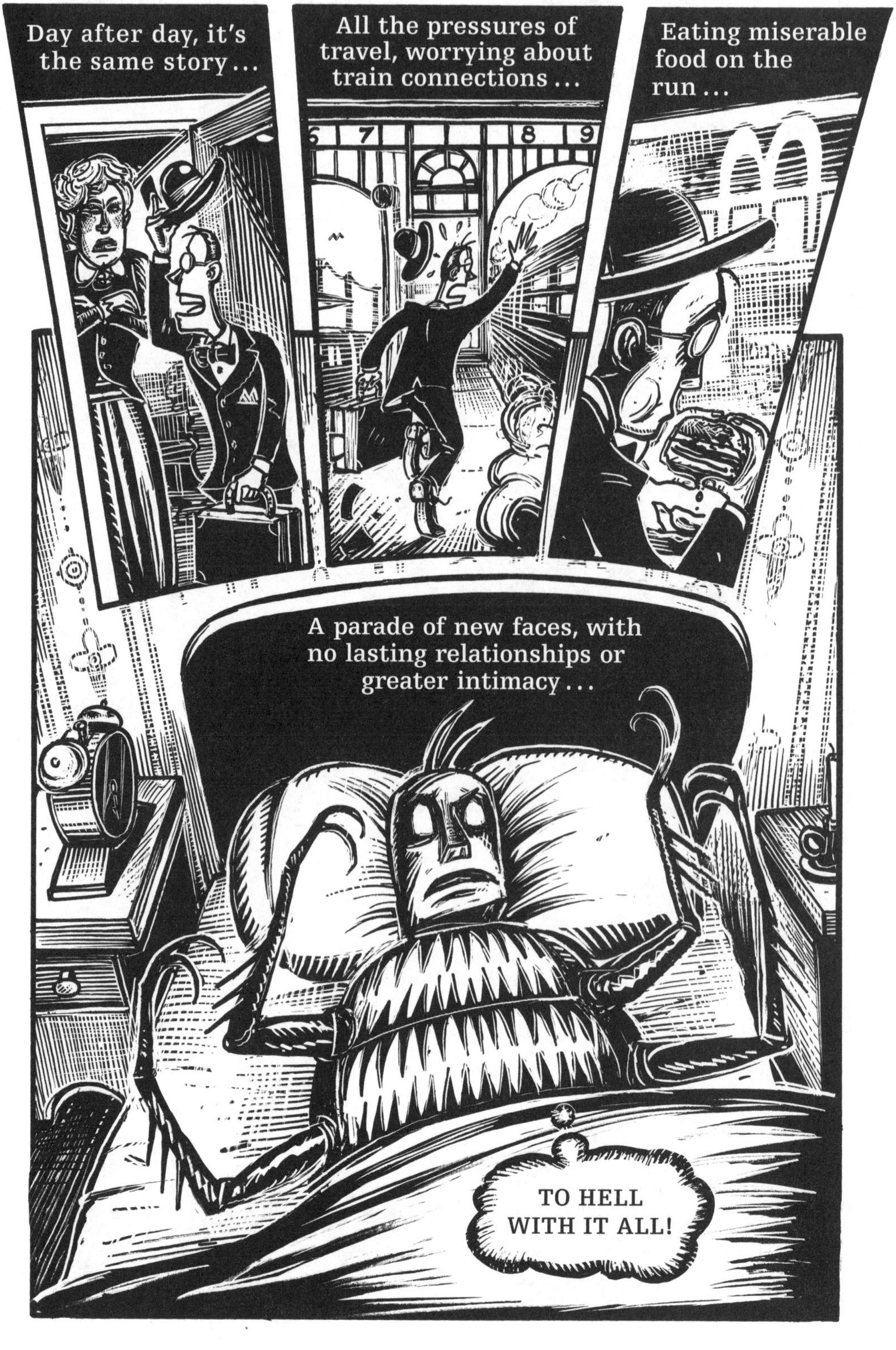
Day after day, it's the same story . . .
All the pressures of travel, worrying about train connections . . .
Eating miserable food on the run . . .
A parade of new faces, with no lasting relationships or greater intimacy . . .
TO HELL WITH IT ALL!

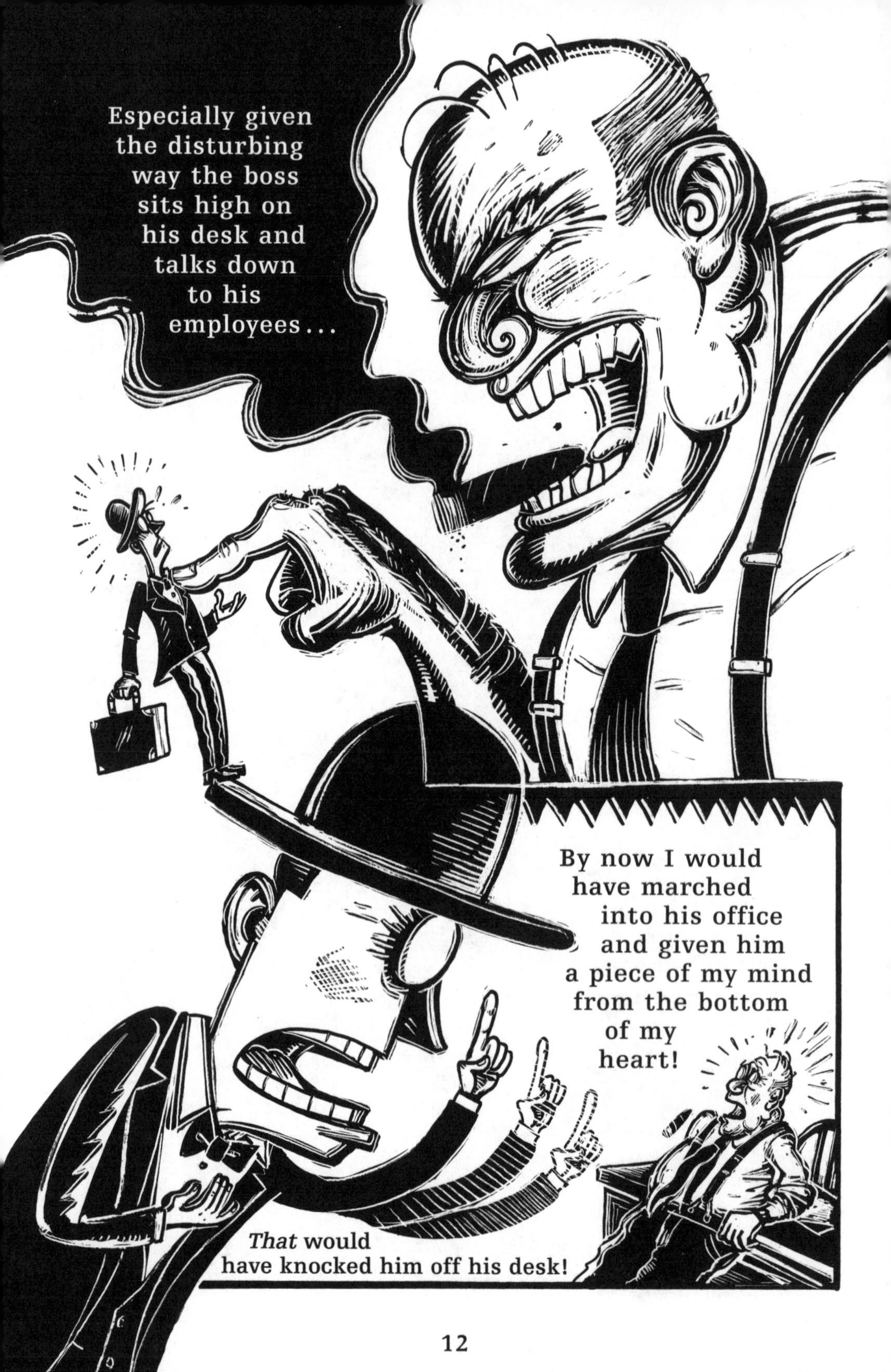
Especially given the disturbing way the boss sits high on his desk and talks down to his employees...
By now I would have marched into his office and given him a piece of my mind from the bottom of my heart!
That would have knocked him off his desk!

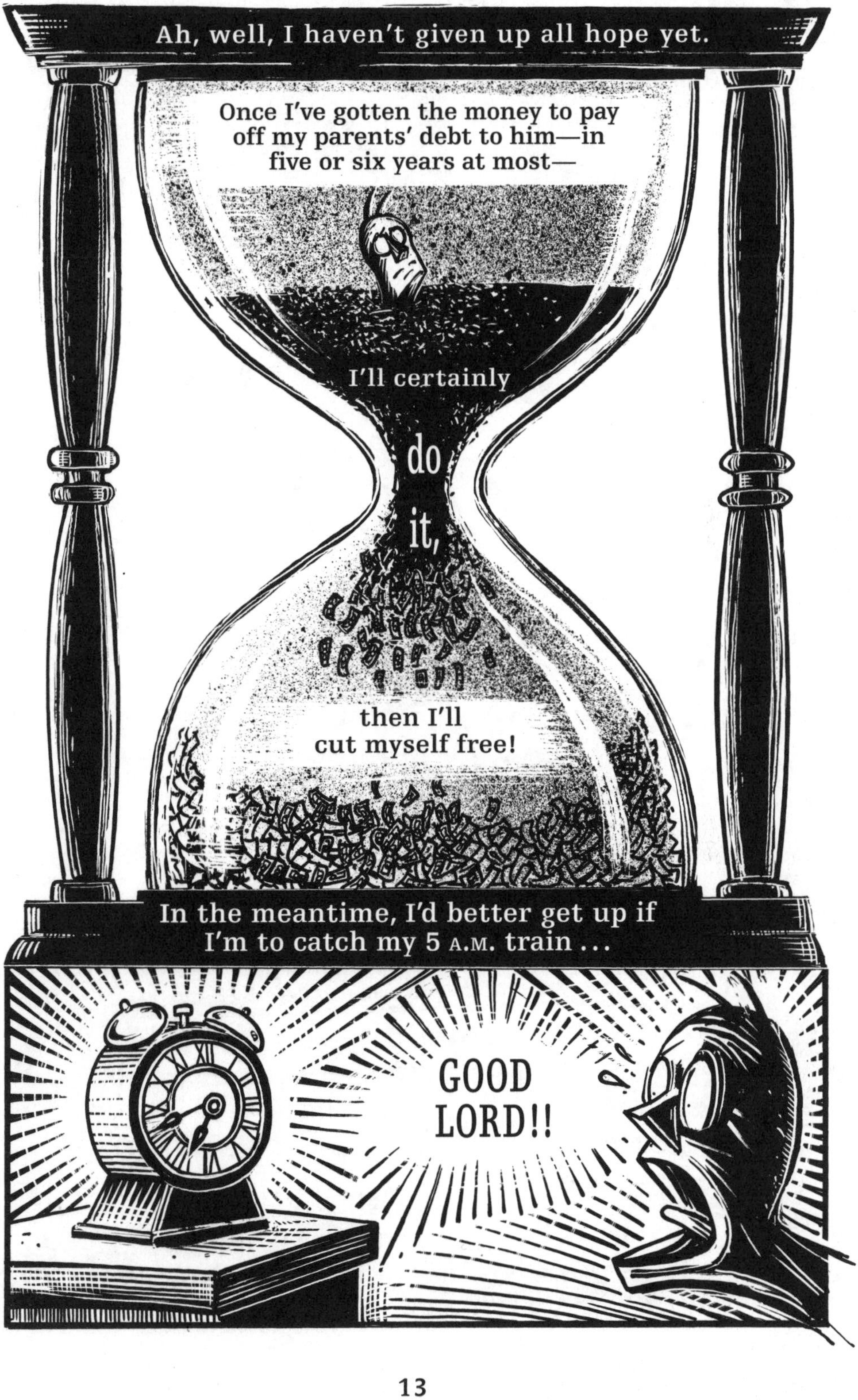
Ah, well, I haven't given up all hope yet.
Once I've gotten the money to pay off my parents' debt to him—in five or six years at most—
I'll certainly
do
it,
then I'll cut myself free!
In the meantime, I'd better get up if I'm to catch my 5 A.M. train . . .
GOOD LORD!!

14

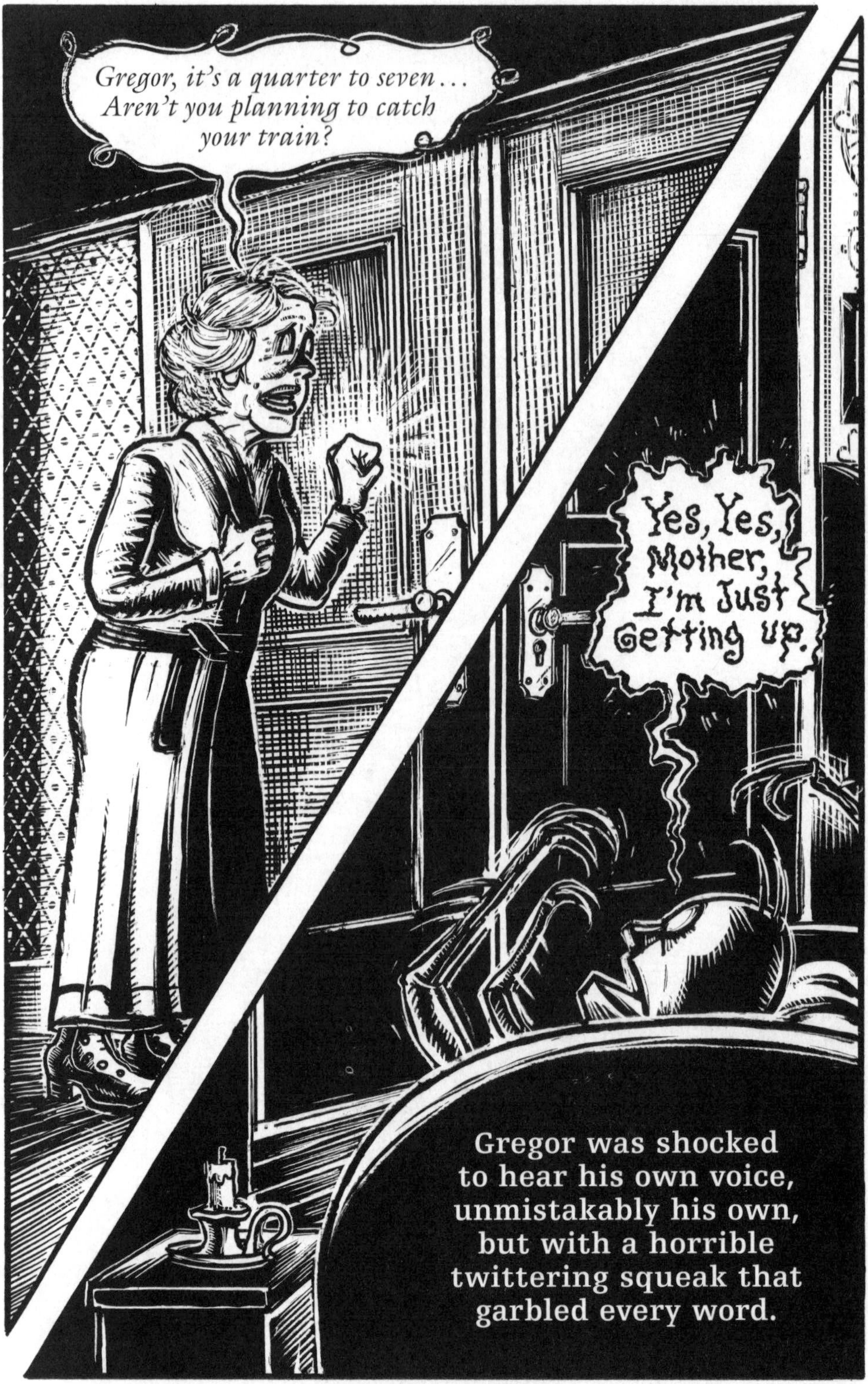
Gregor, it's a quarter to seven... Aren't you planning to catch your train?
Yes, Yes, Mother, I'm Just Getting up.
Gregor was shocked to hear his own voice, unmistakably his own, but with a horrible twittering squeak that garbled every word.

The change in Gregor's voice must have been muffled by the wooden door because his mother was reassured and shuffled off. However, their little exchange made his father and sister aware that Gregor had not, as they assumed, left for work.

Gregor, it's Grete, are you alright?

Do you need *anything?*

Please, Gregor, open the door.

But Gregor had no intention of unlocking the door and felt thankful for the habit he had acquired as a traveling salesman of bolting it at night, even when he was at home.

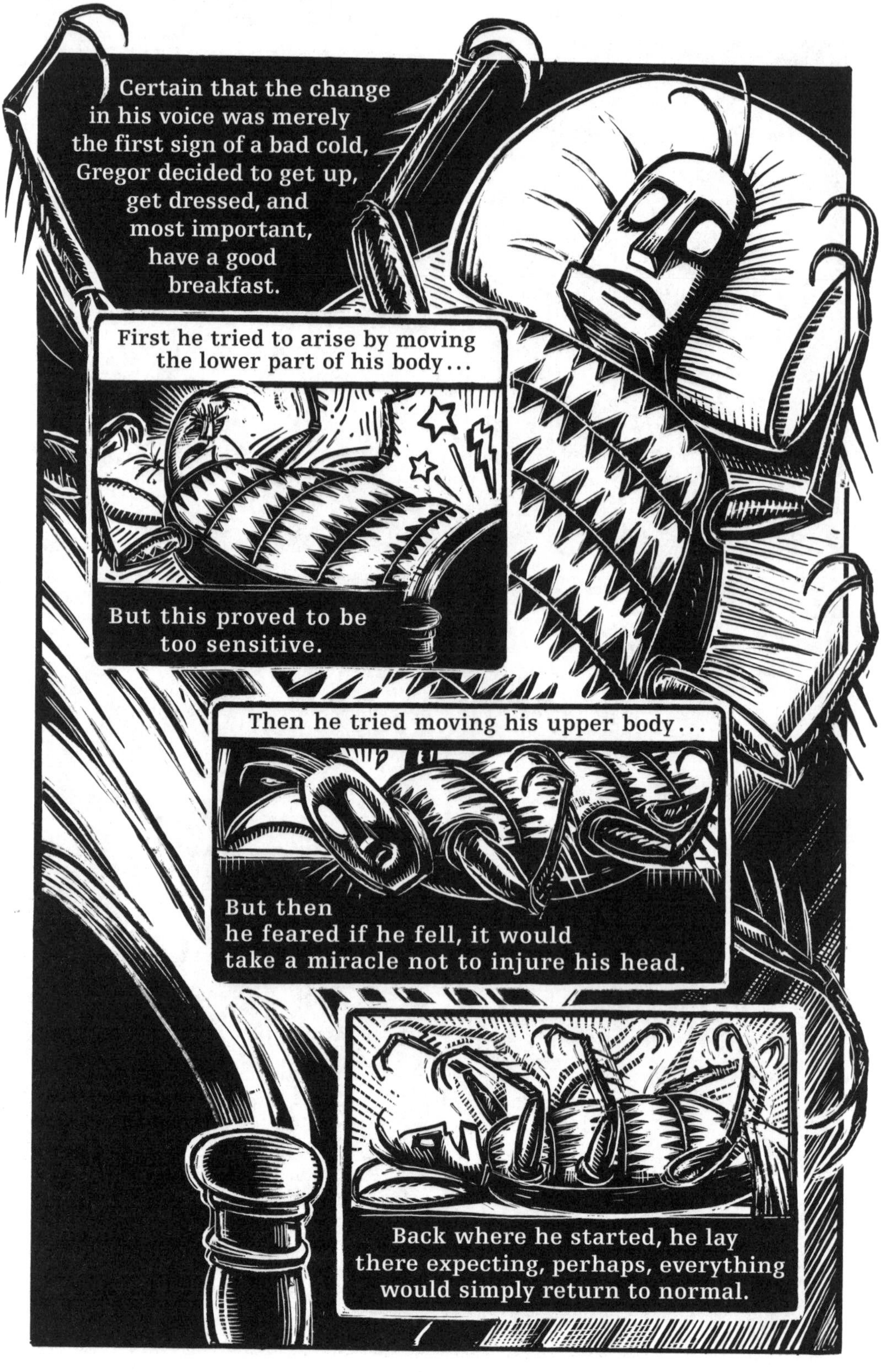

Certain that the change in his voice was merely the first sign of a bad cold, Gregor decided to get up, get dressed, and most important, have a good breakfast.
First he tried to arise by moving the lower part of his body...
But this proved to be too sensitive.
Then he tried moving his upper body...
But then he feared if he fell, it would take a miracle not to injure his head.
Back where he started, he lay there expecting, perhaps, everything would simply return to normal.

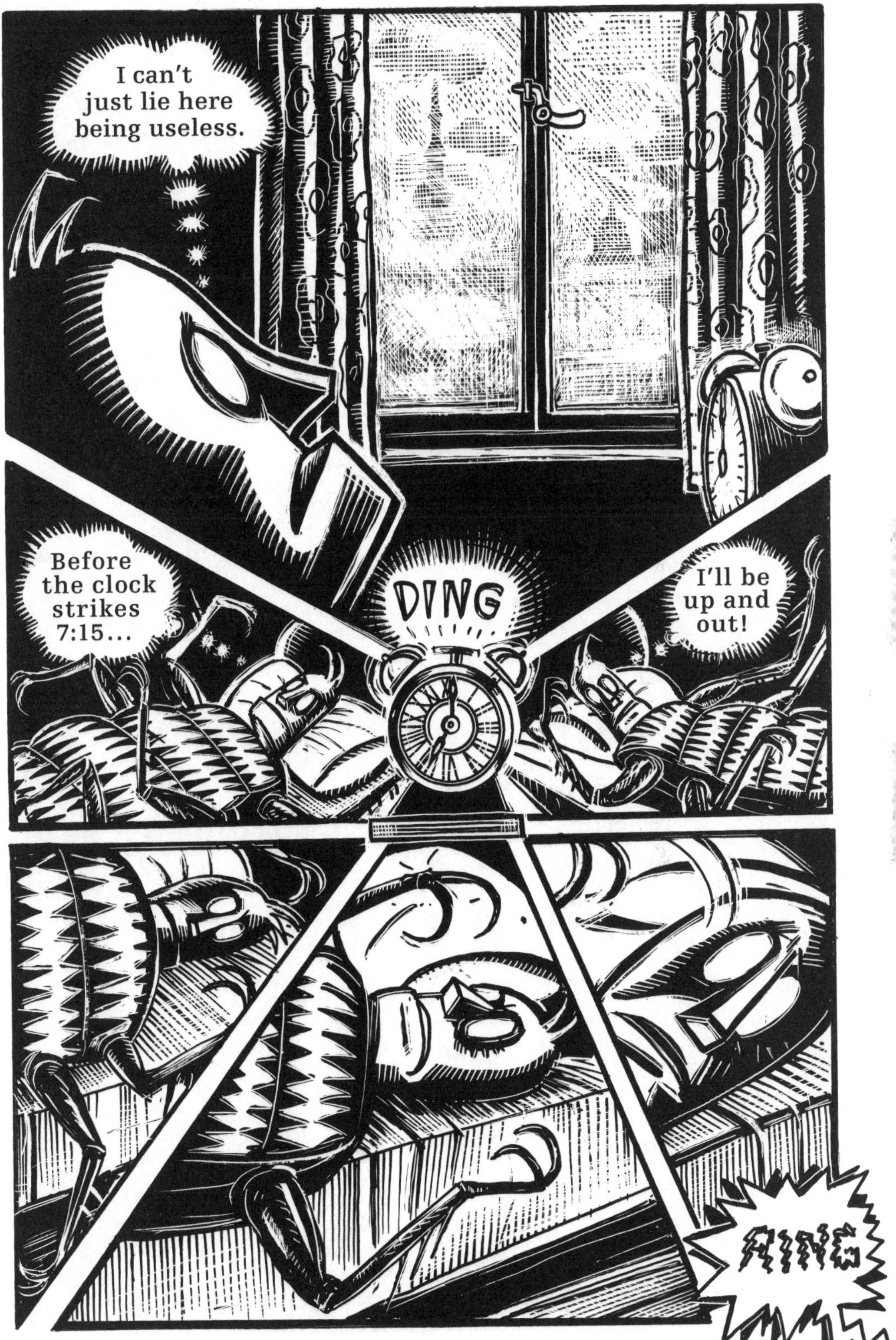
I can't just lie here being useless.
Before the clock strikes 7:15...
DING
I'll be up and out!
RING

20

22

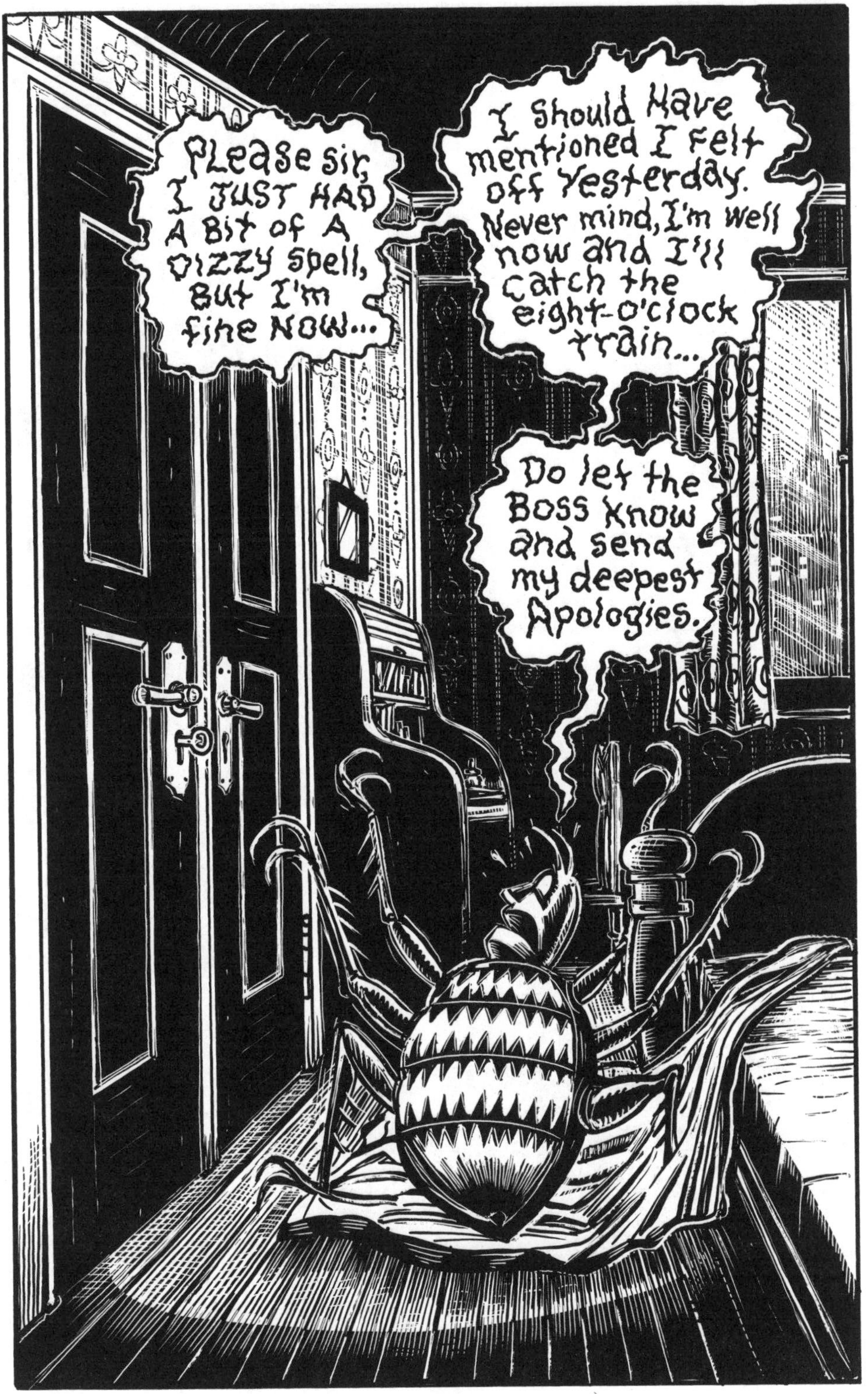
Please sir, I JUST HAD A Bit of A DIZZY spell, But I'm fine NOW...
I should Have mentioned I Felt off yesterday. Never mind, I'm well now and I'll catch the eight-o'clock train...
Do let the Boss Know and send my deepest Apologies.

24

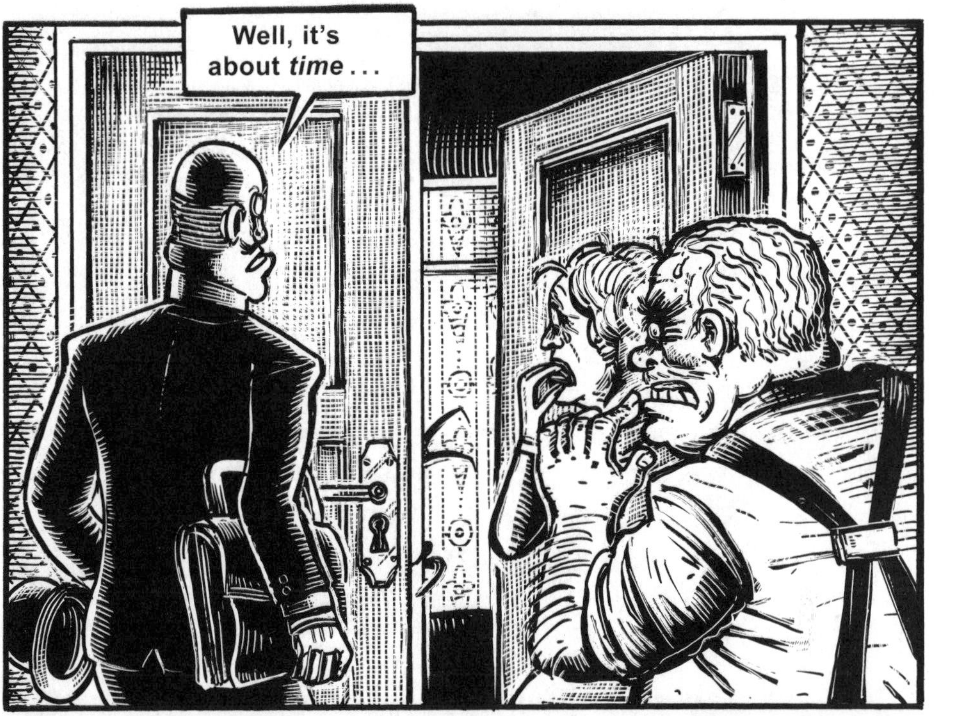
Well, it's about *time* . . .

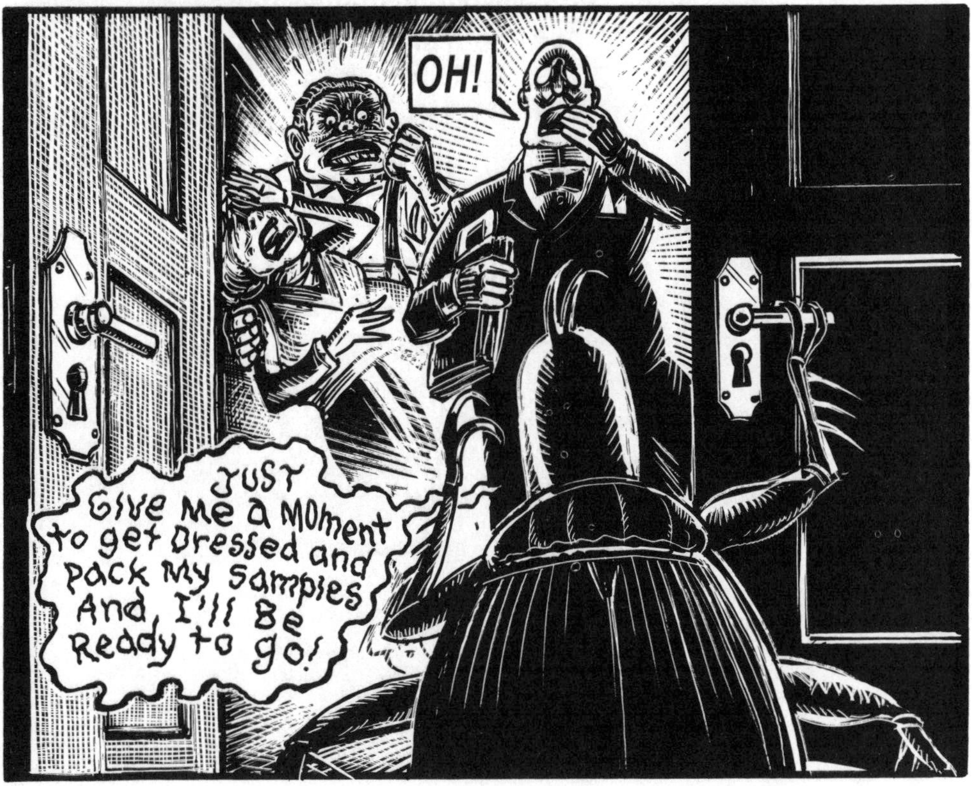
OH!
JUST GIVE ME A MOMENT TO GET DRESSED AND PACK MY SAMPLES AND, I'LL BE READY TO GO!

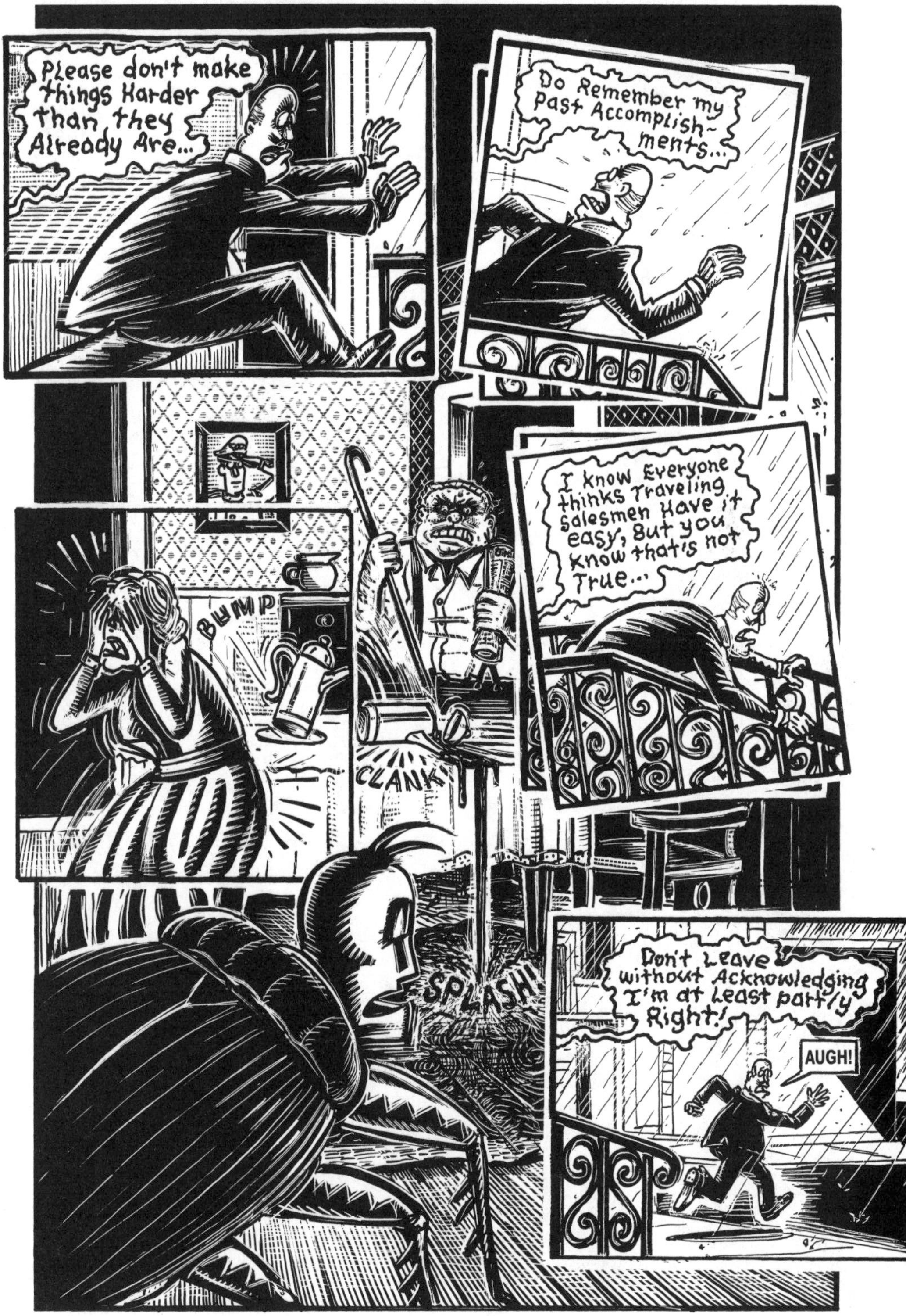
Please don't make things Harder than they Already Are...
Do Remember my Past Accomplish-ments...
BUMP
CLANK
I know Everyone thinks Traveling Salesmen Have it easy, But you know that's not True...
SPLASH!
Don't Leave without Acknowledging I'm at Least partly Right!
AUGH!

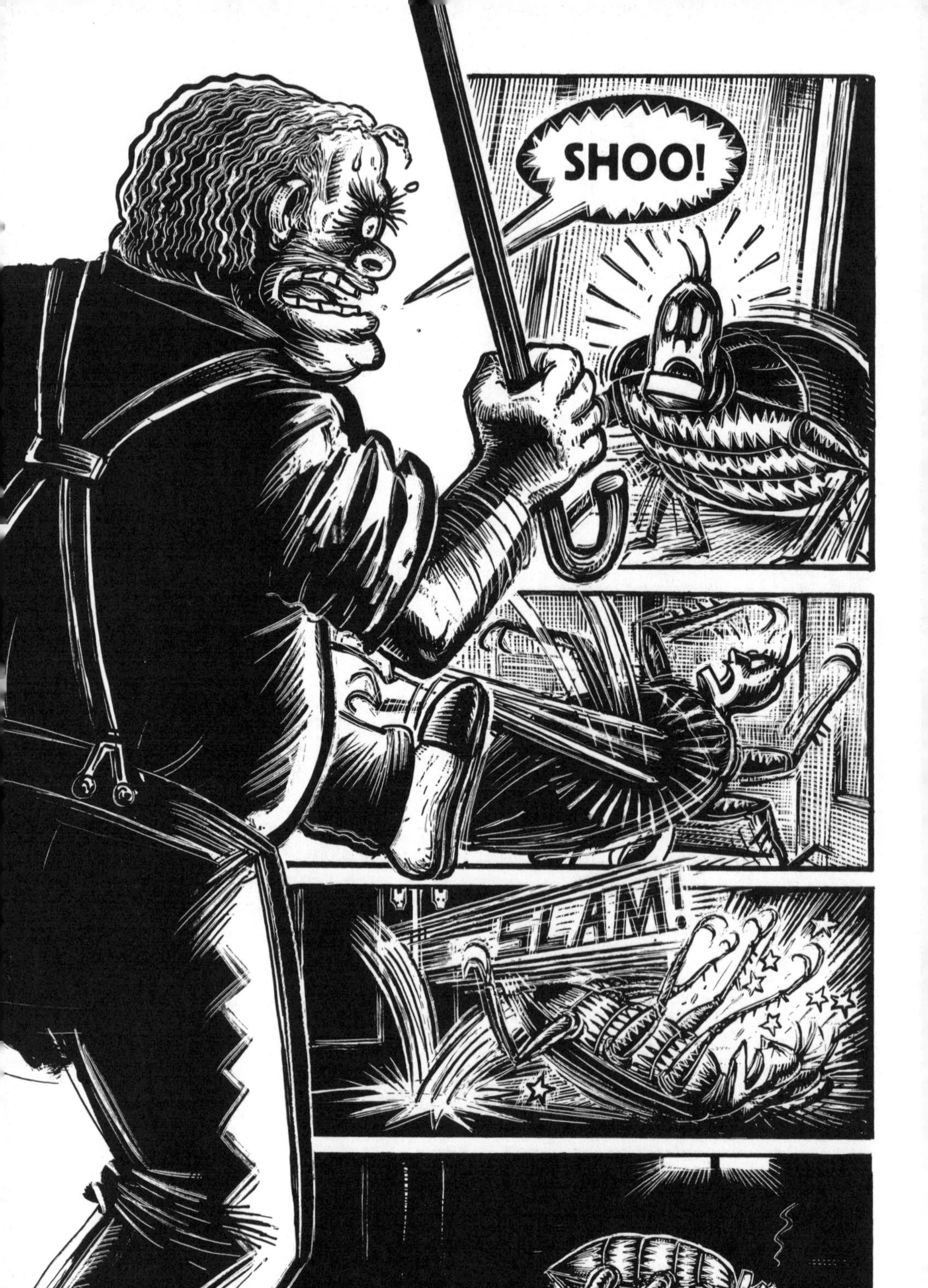
SHOO!
SLAM!

II

By the time Gregor awoke from his coma-like sleep, it was dusk. Though he could see through a crack in the door that their pleasant apartment was not empty, all was silent.

As he lay there, Gregor thought about how proud he felt to have provided this comfortable home for his sister and parents.

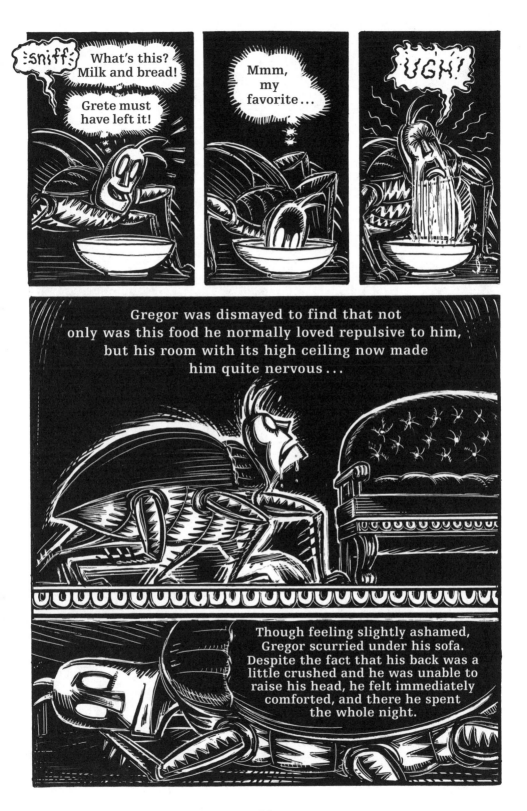

31

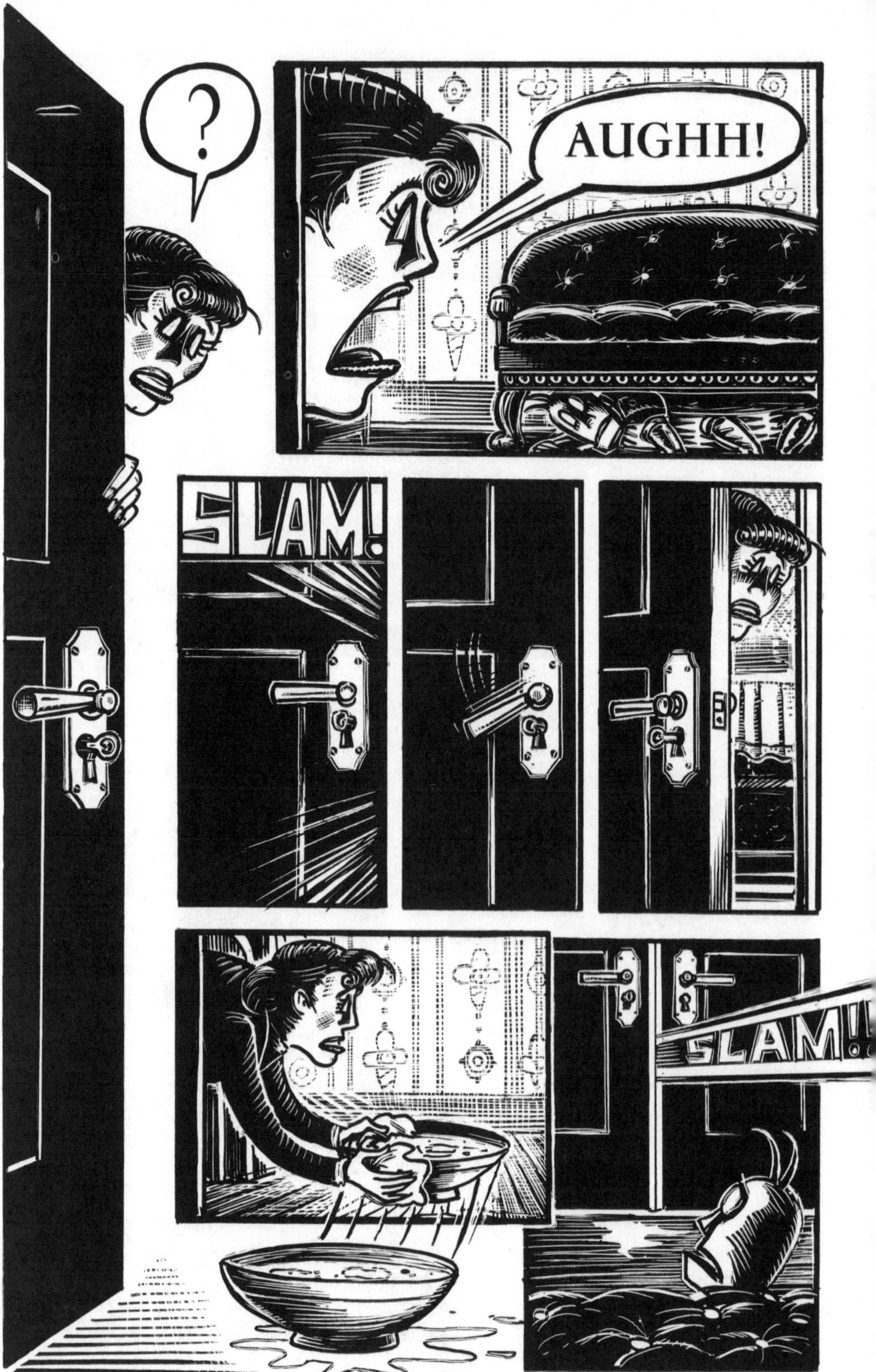
?
AUGHH!
SLAM!
SLAM!!

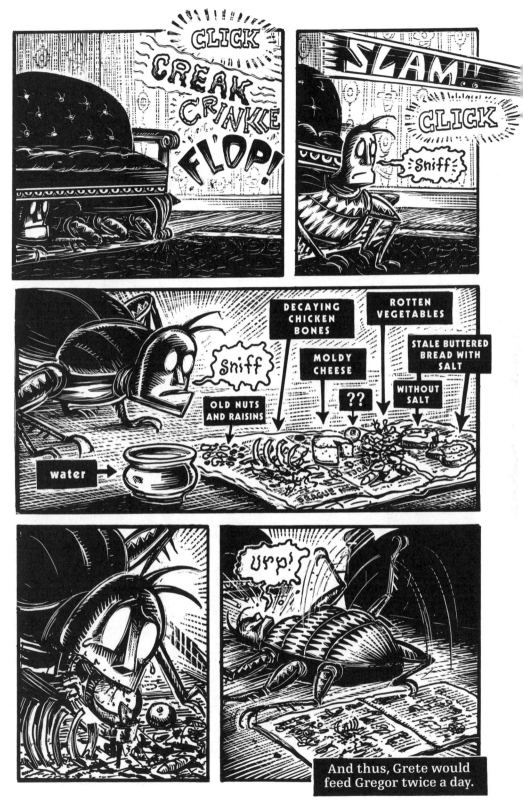

And thus, Grete would feed Gregor twice a day.

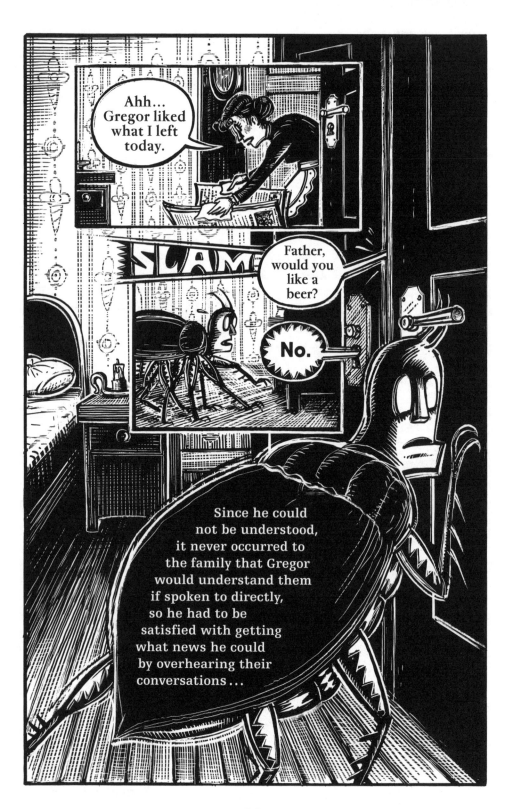

34

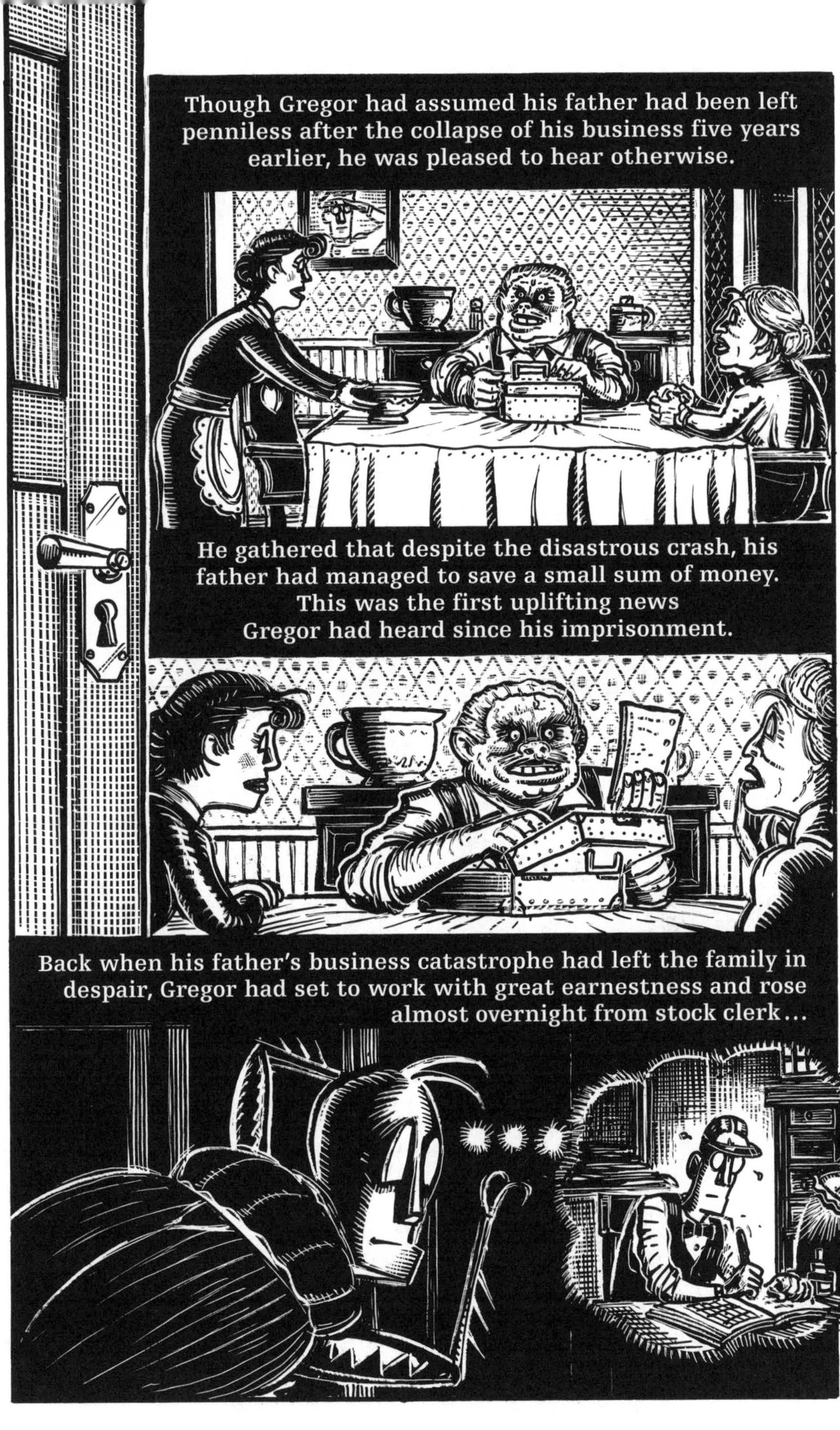
Though Gregor had assumed his father had been left penniless after the collapse of his business five years earlier, he was pleased to hear otherwise.
He gathered that despite the disastrous crash, his father had managed to save a small sum of money. This was the first uplifting news Gregor had heard since his imprisonment.
Back when his father's business catastrophe had left the family in despair, Gregor had set to work with great earnestness and rose almost overnight from stock clerk...

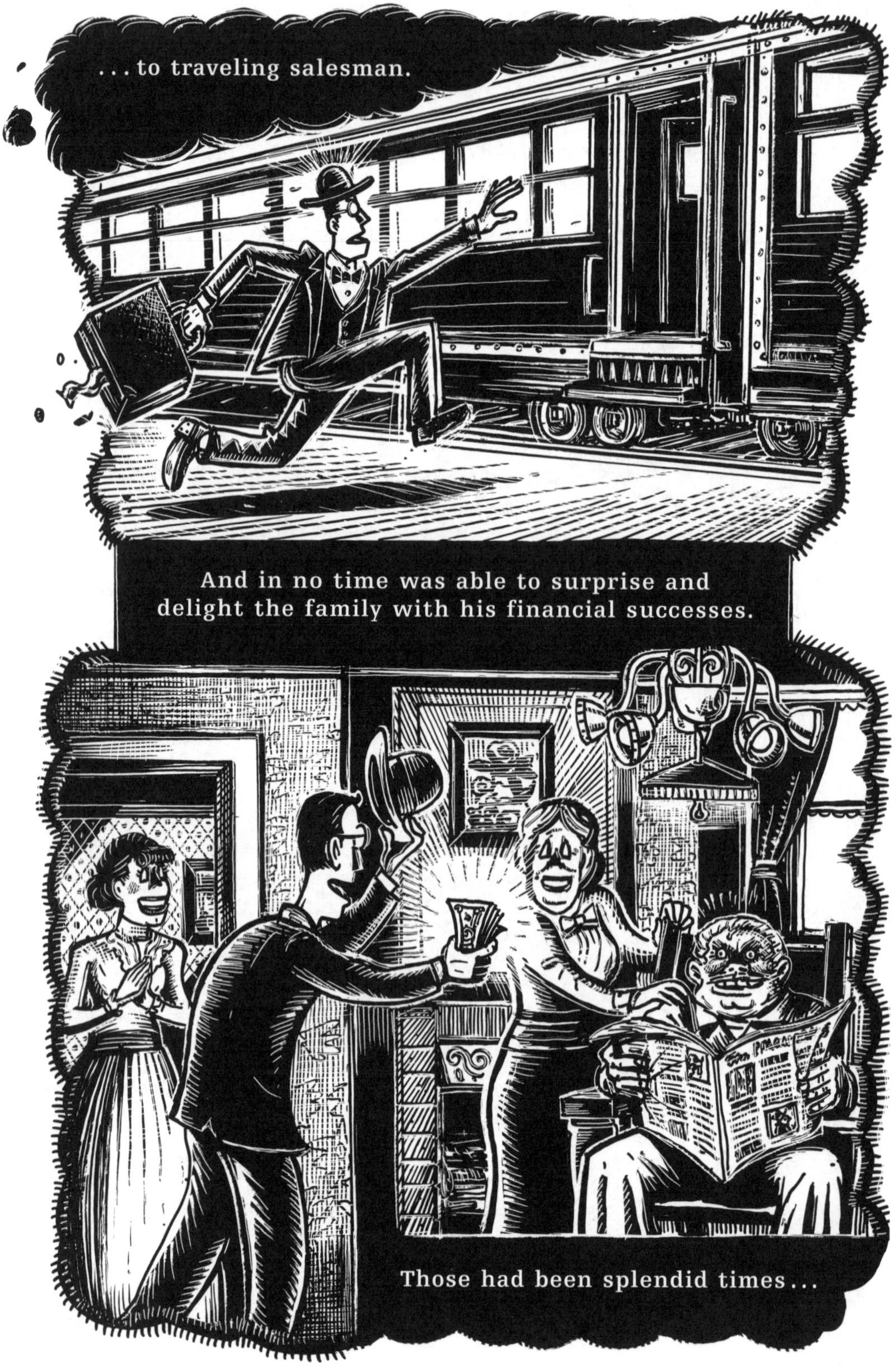
. . . to traveling salesman.
And in no time was able to surprise and delight the family with his financial successes.
Those had been splendid times . . .

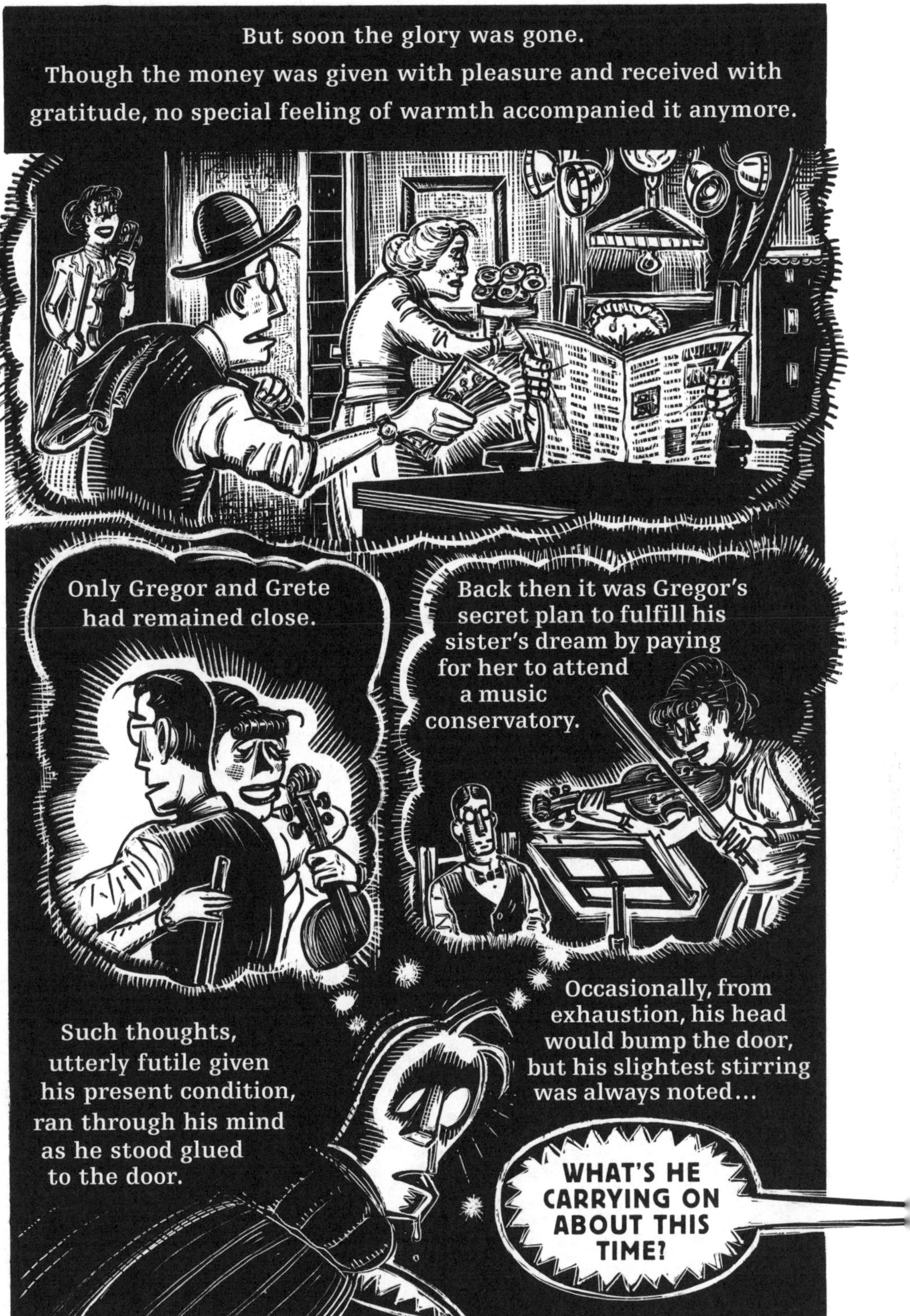
But soon the glory was gone.
Though the money was given with pleasure and received with gratitude, no special feeling of warmth accompanied it anymore.
Only Gregor and Grete had remained close.
Back then it was Gregor's secret plan to fulfill his sister's dream by paying for her to attend a music conservatory.
Such thoughts, utterly futile given his present condition, ran through his mind as he stood glued to the door.
Occasionally, from exhaustion, his head would bump the door, but his slightest stirring was always noted...
WHAT'S HE CARRYING ON ABOUT THIS TIME?

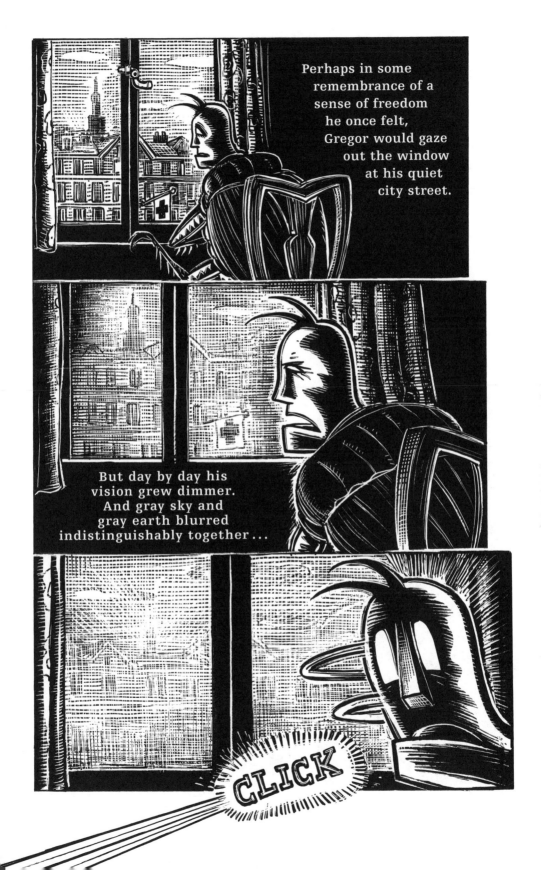

40

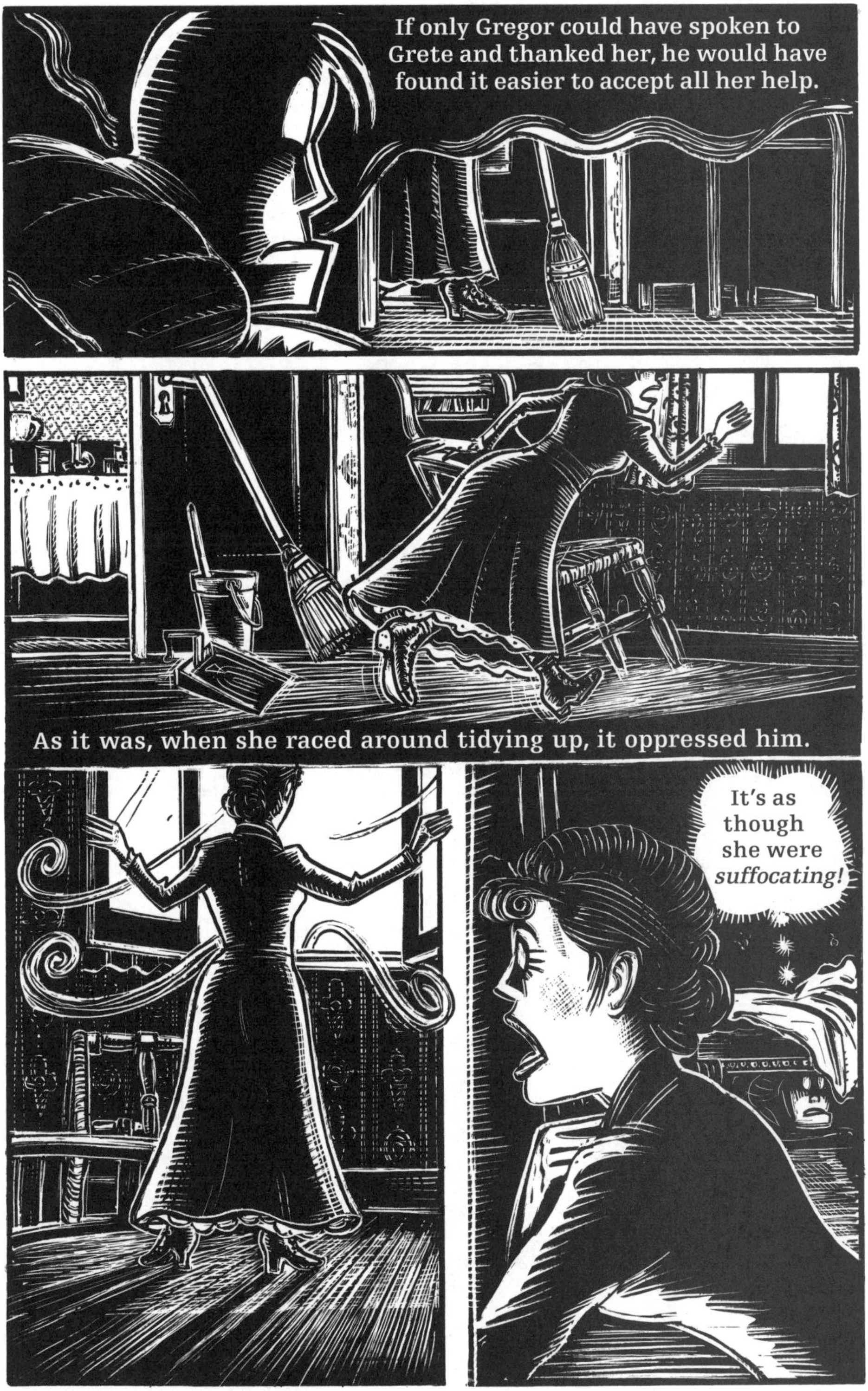
If only Gregor could have spoken to Grete and thanked her, he would have found it easier to accept all her help.
As it was, when she raced around tidying up, it oppressed him.
It's as though she were *suffocating!*

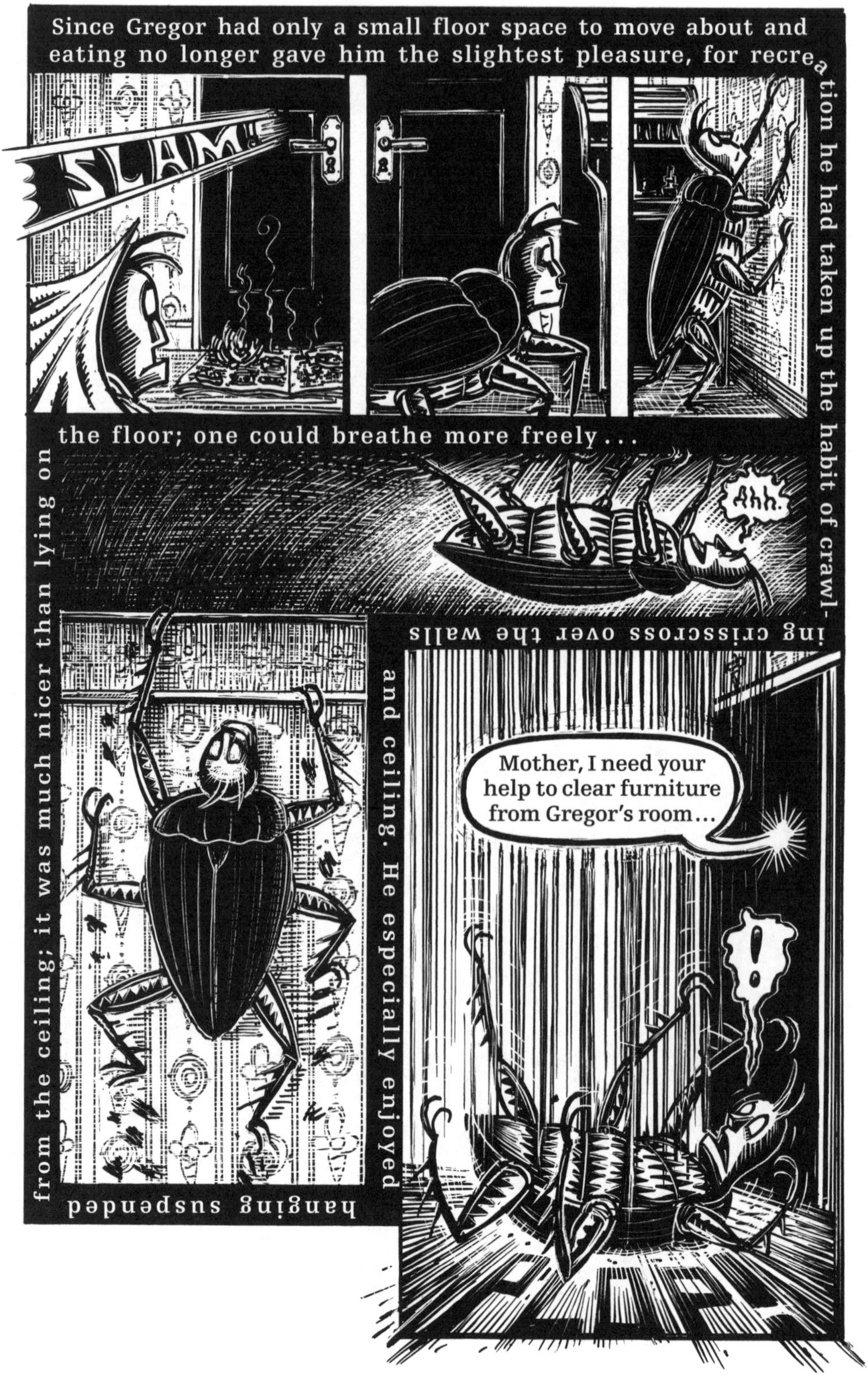
Since Gregor had only a small floor space to move about and eating no longer gave him the slightest pleasure, for recreation he had taken up the habit of crawling crisscross over the walls
SLAM!
and ceiling. He especially enjoyed hanging suspended from the ceiling; it was much nicer than lying on the floor; one could breathe more freely . . .
Ahh.
Mother, I need your help to clear furniture from Gregor's room . . .
!

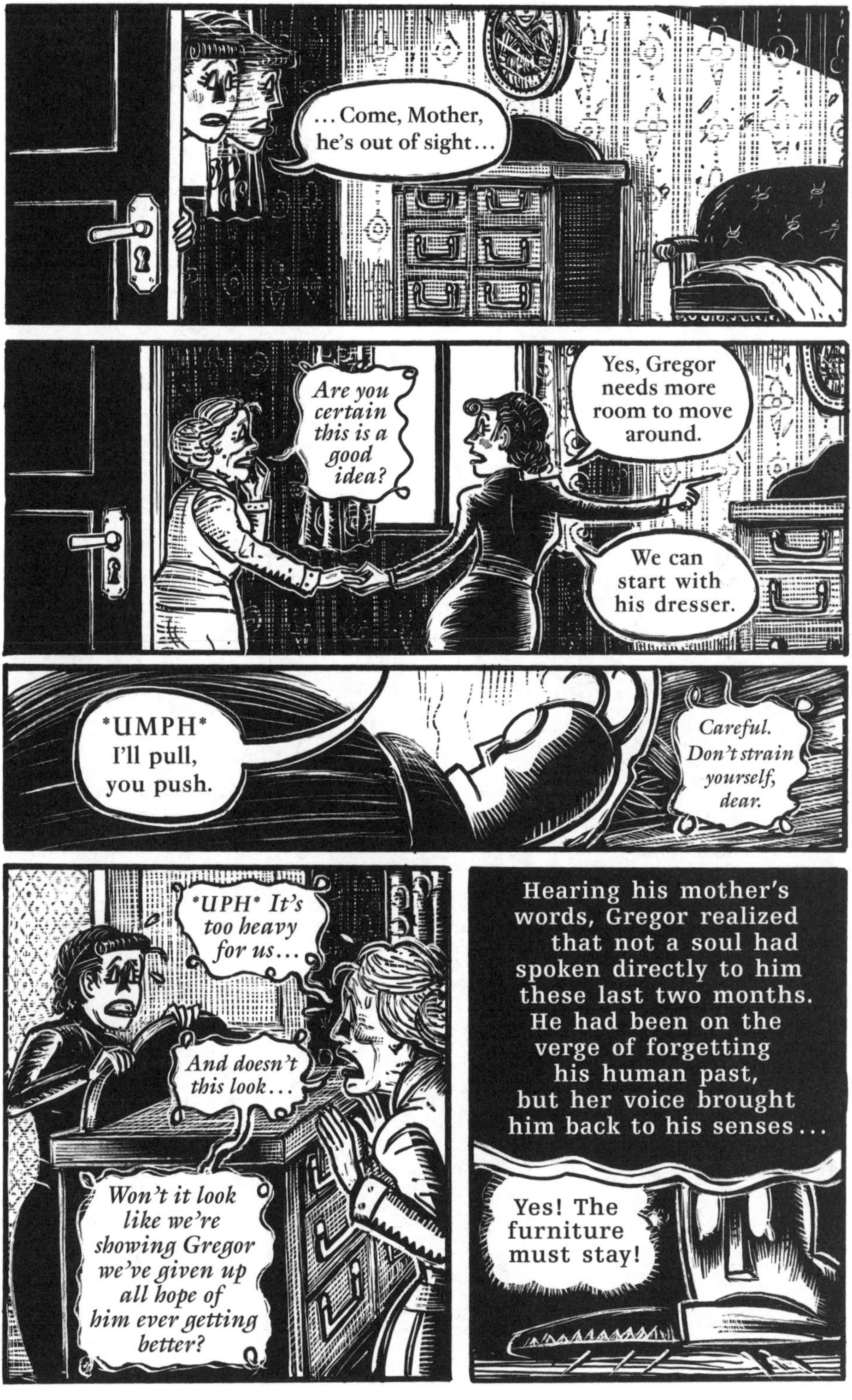
...Come, Mother, he's out of sight...
Are you certain this is a good idea?
Yes, Gregor needs more room to move around.
We can start with his dresser.
UMPH I'll pull, you push.
Careful. Don't strain yourself, dear.
UPH It's too heavy for us...
And doesn't this look...
Won't it look like we're showing Gregor we've given up all hope of him ever getting better?
Hearing his mother's words, Gregor realized that not a soul had spoken directly to him these last two months. He had been on the verge of forgetting his human past, but her voice brought him back to his senses...
Yes! The furniture must stay!

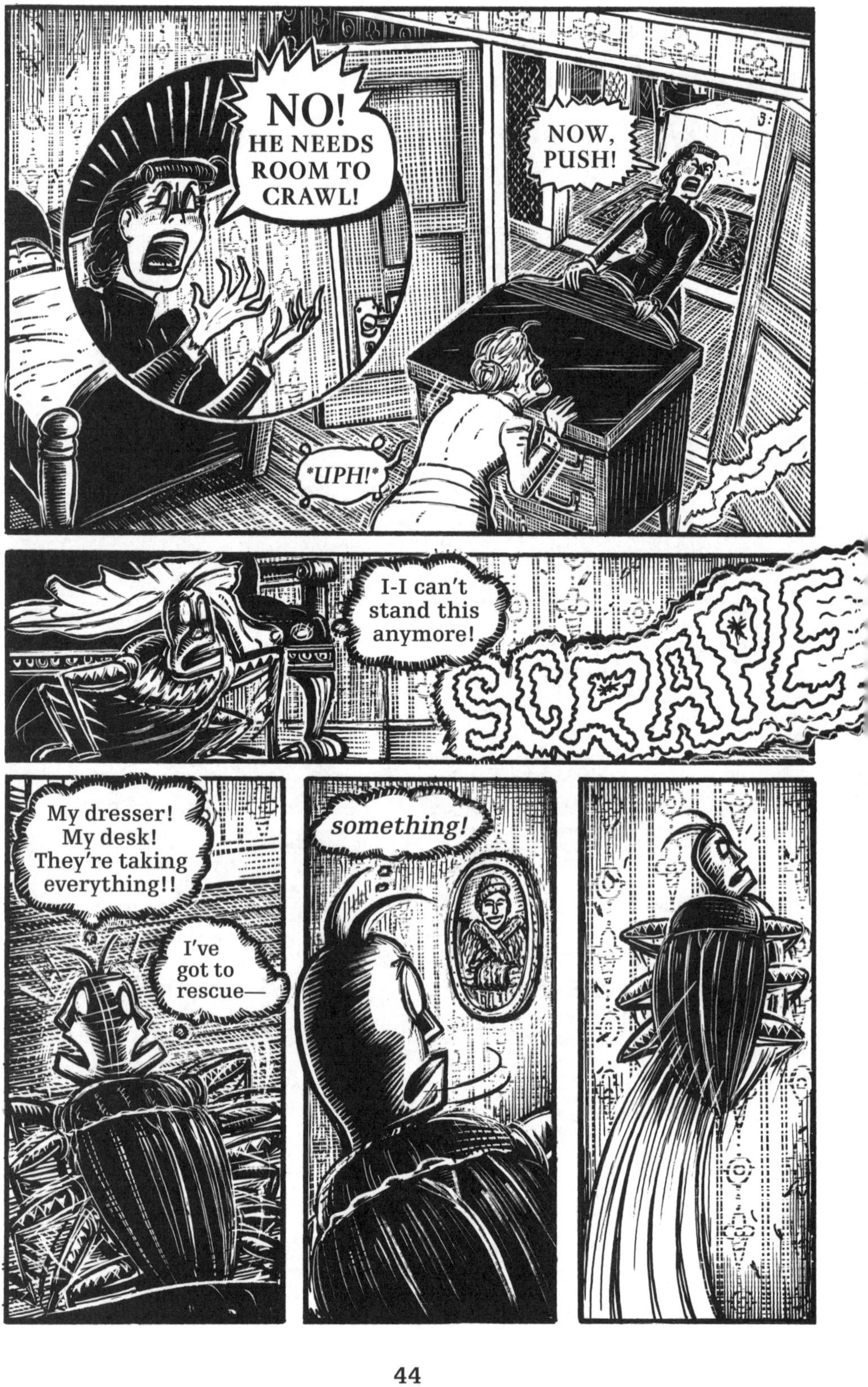
NO!
HE NEEDS ROOM TO CRAWL!
NOW, PUSH!
UPH!
I-I can't stand this anymore!
SCRAPE
My dresser! My desk! They're taking everything!!
I've got to rescue—
something!

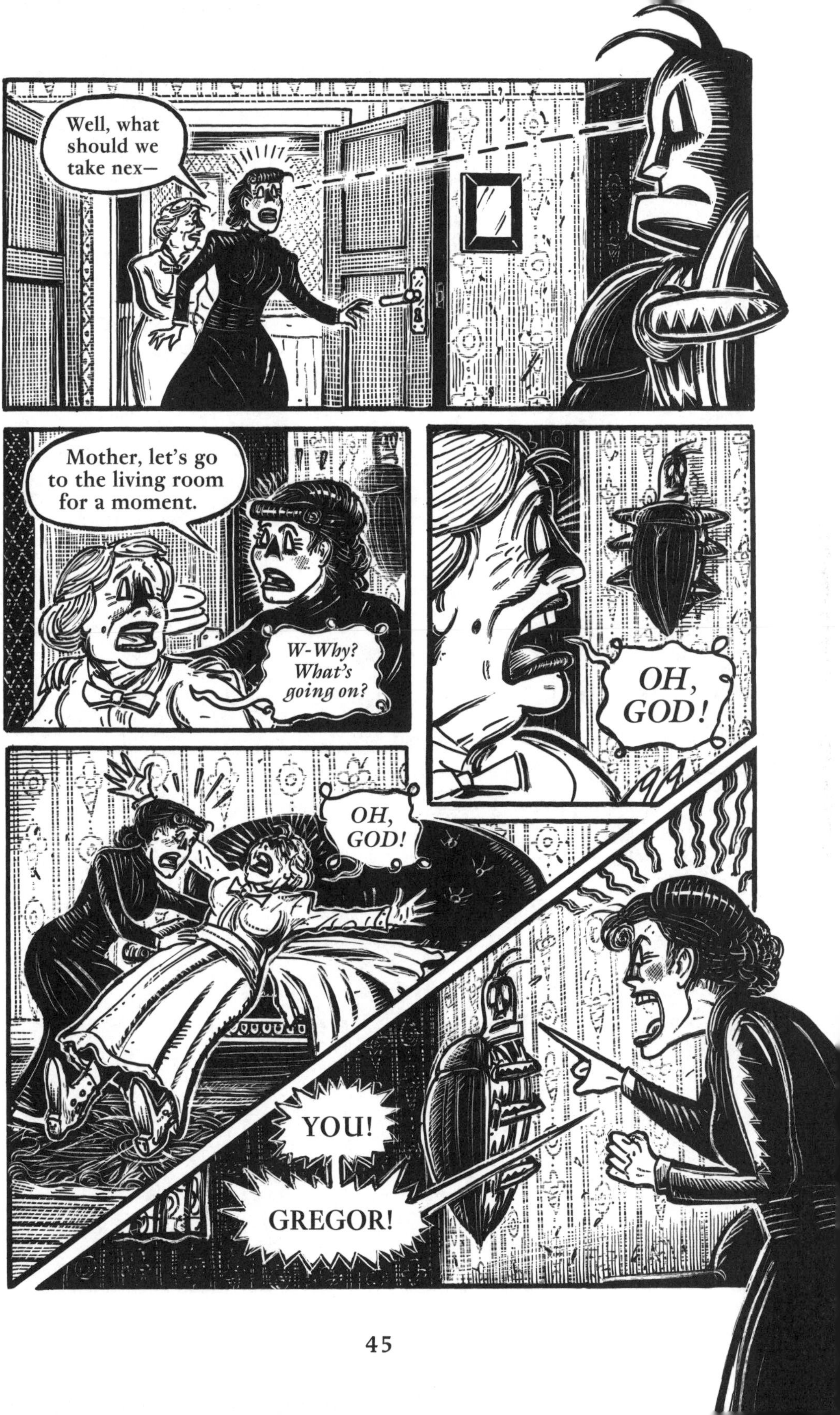

Well, what should we take nex—
Mother, let's go to the living room for a moment.
W-Why? What's going on?
OH, GOD!
OH, GOD!
YOU!
GREGOR!

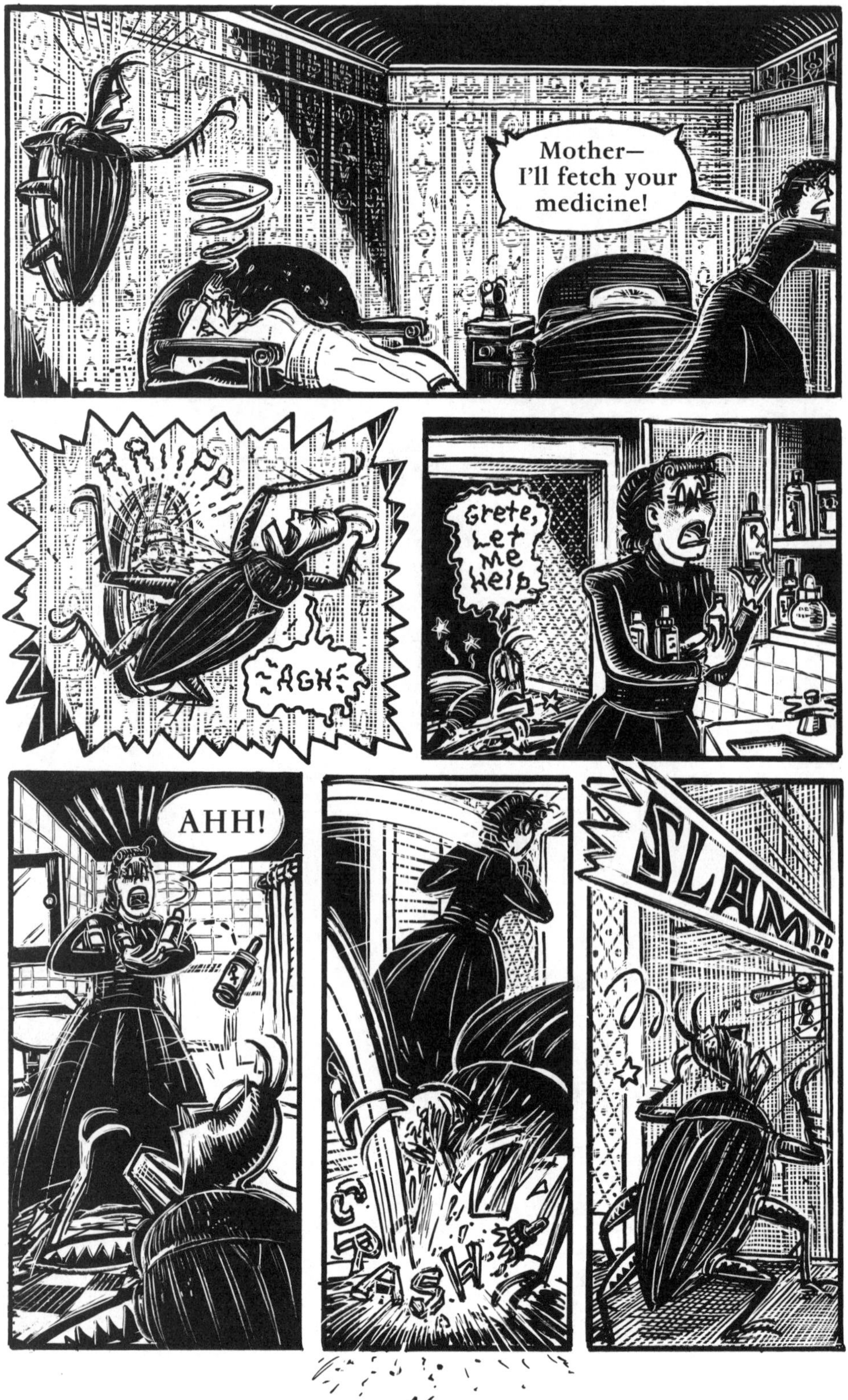
Mother—
I'll fetch your medicine!
RRIIPP
AGH
Grete, Let me Help
AHH!
CRASH
SLAM!!

47

C-Could this be *Father??*
The same tired old man...?
But Gregor did not dwell on this reflection for he had known from the very first day of his new life that his father considered only the harshest measures suitable for dealing with him...

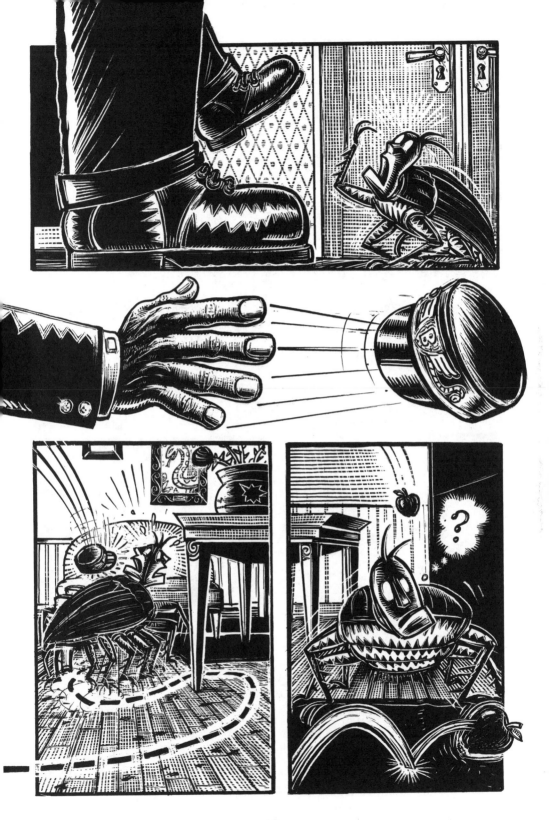

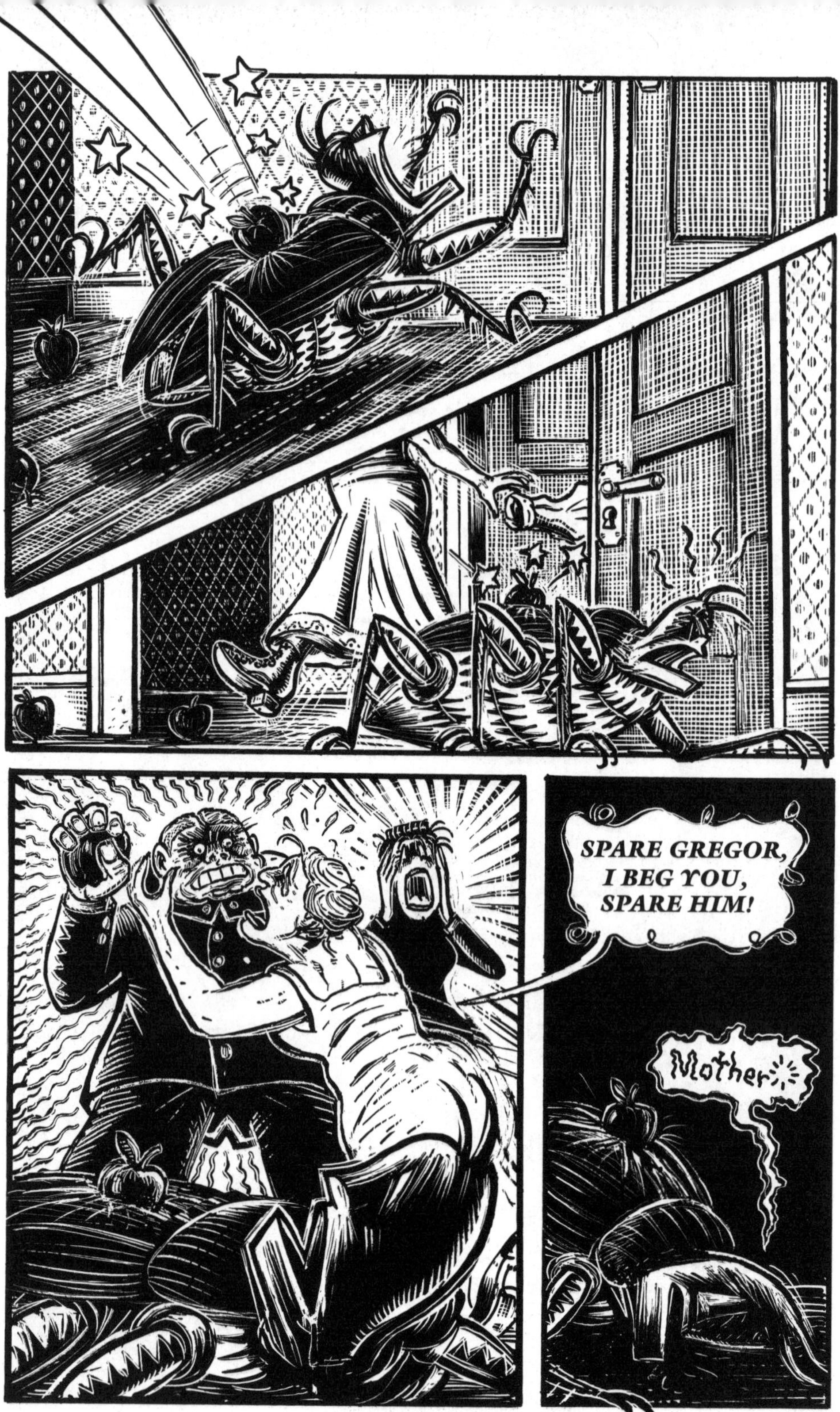
SPARE GREGOR, I BEG YOU, SPARE HIM!
Mother

III

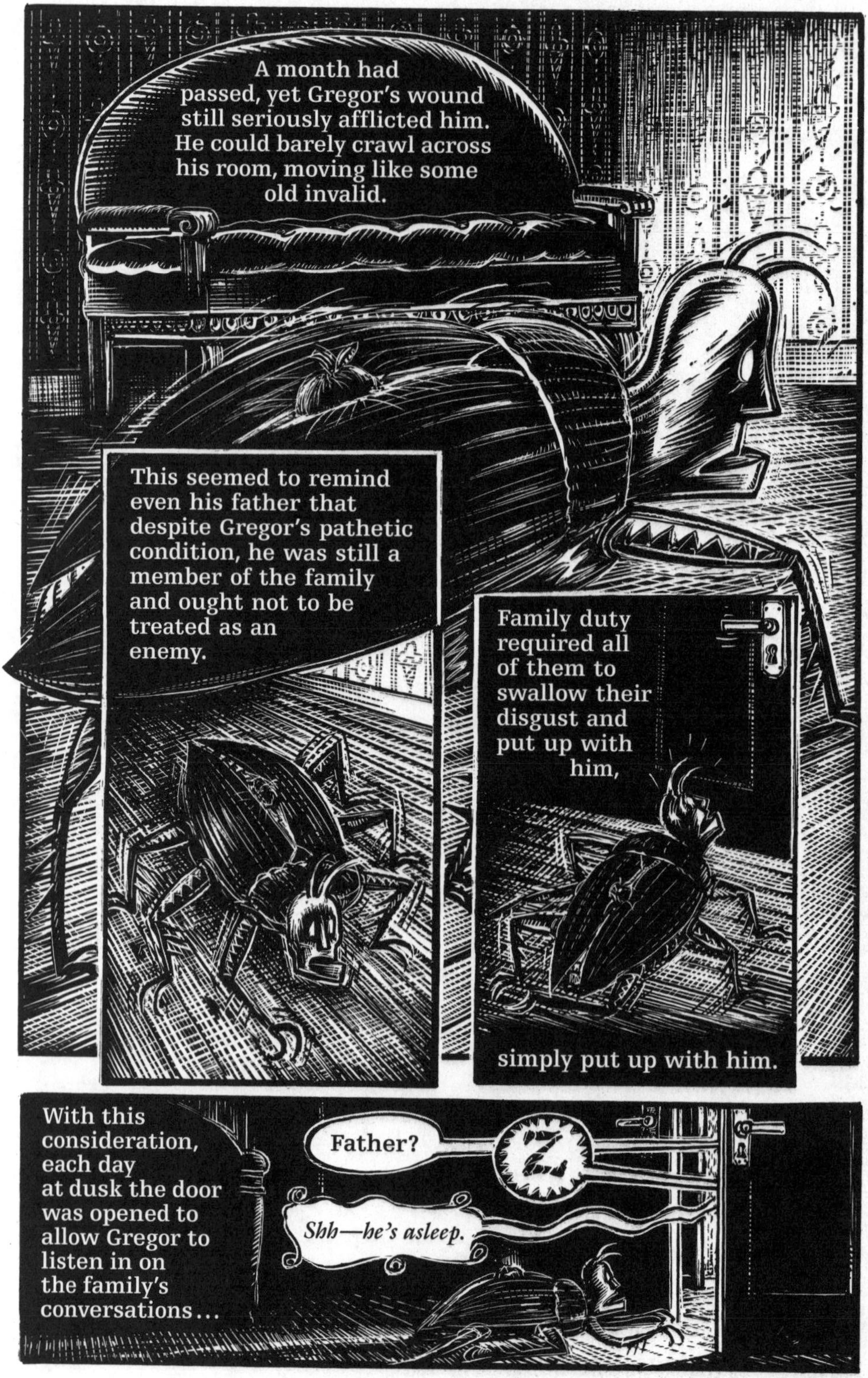

A month had passed, yet Gregor's wound still seriously afflicted him. He could barely crawl across his room, moving like some old invalid.
This seemed to remind even his father that despite Gregor's pathetic condition, he was still a member of the family and ought not to be treated as an enemy.
Family duty required all of them to swallow their disgust and put up with him,
simply put up with him.
With this consideration, each day at dusk the door was opened to allow Gregor to listen in on the family's conversations...
Father?
Z
Shh—he's asleep.

53

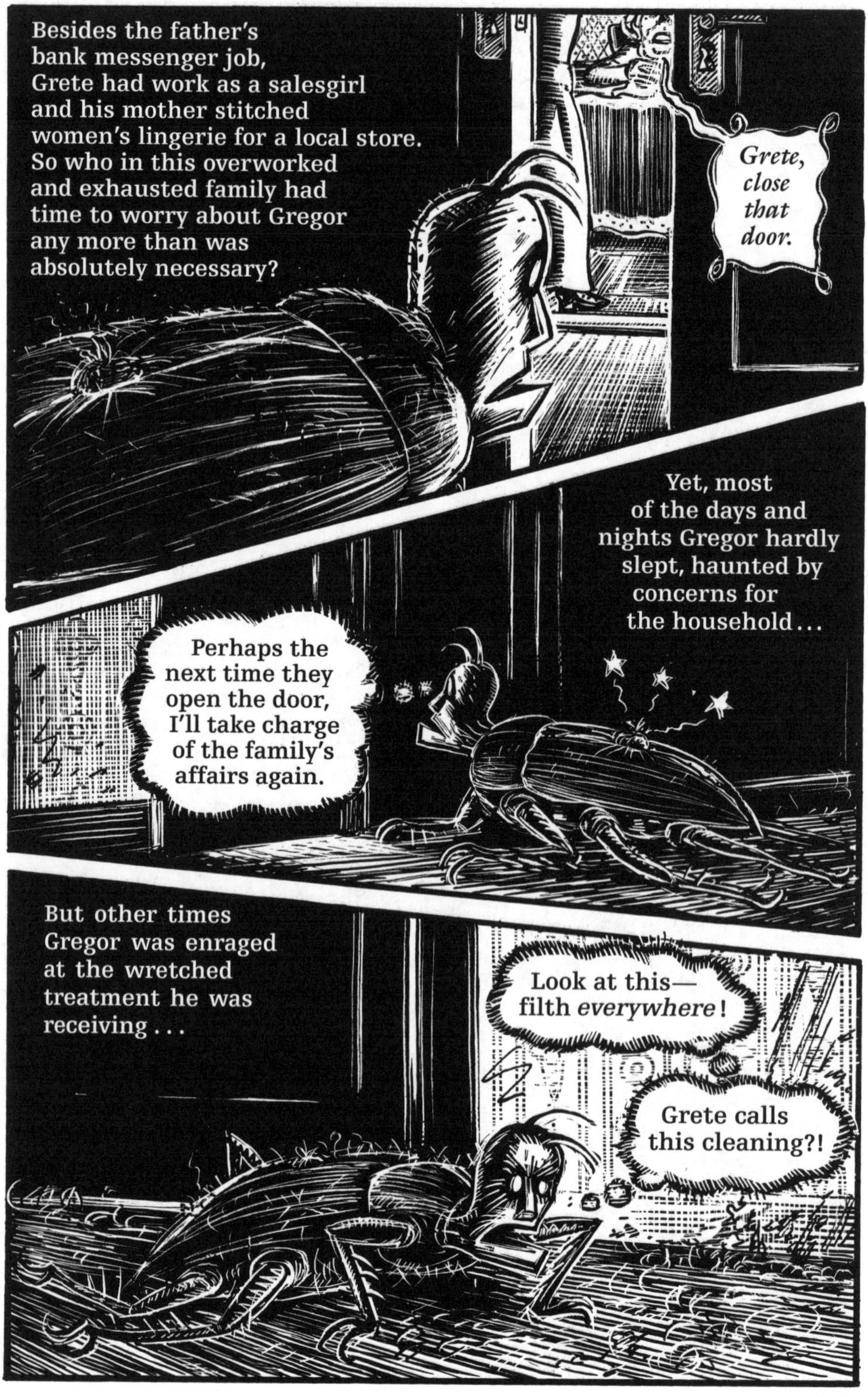
Besides the father's bank messenger job, Grete had work as a salesgirl and his mother stitched women's lingerie for a local store. So who in this overworked and exhausted family had time to worry about Gregor any more than was absolutely necessary?
Grete, close that door.
Yet, most of the days and nights Gregor hardly slept, haunted by concerns for the household...
Perhaps the next time they open the door, I'll take charge of the family's affairs again.
But other times Gregor was enraged at the wretched treatment he was receiving...
Look at this— filth *everywhere*!
Grete calls this cleaning?!

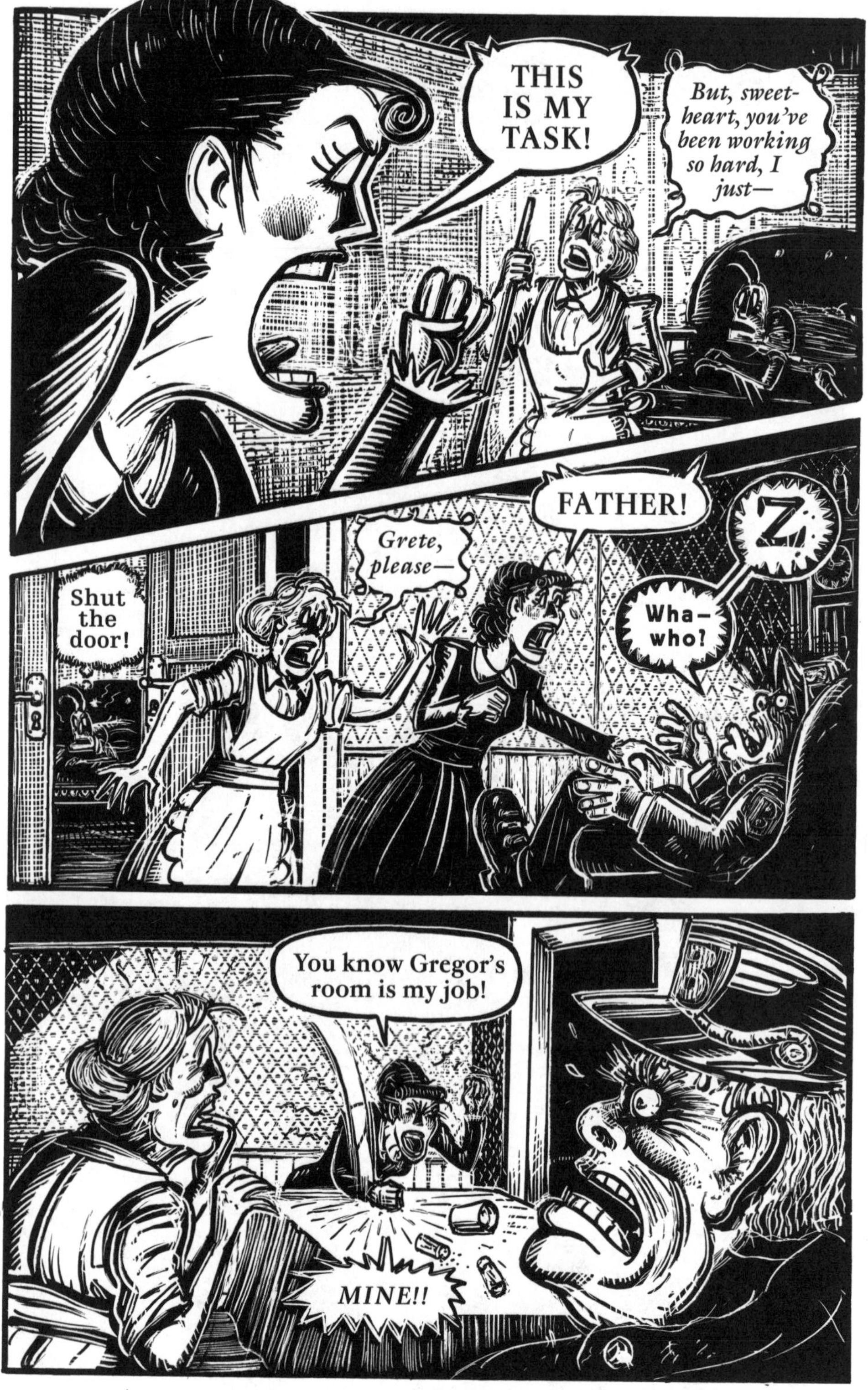
THIS IS MY TASK!
But, sweet-heart, you've been working so hard, I just—
Shut the door!
Grete, please—
FATHER!
Z
Wha-who?
You know Gregor's room is my job!
MINE!!

57

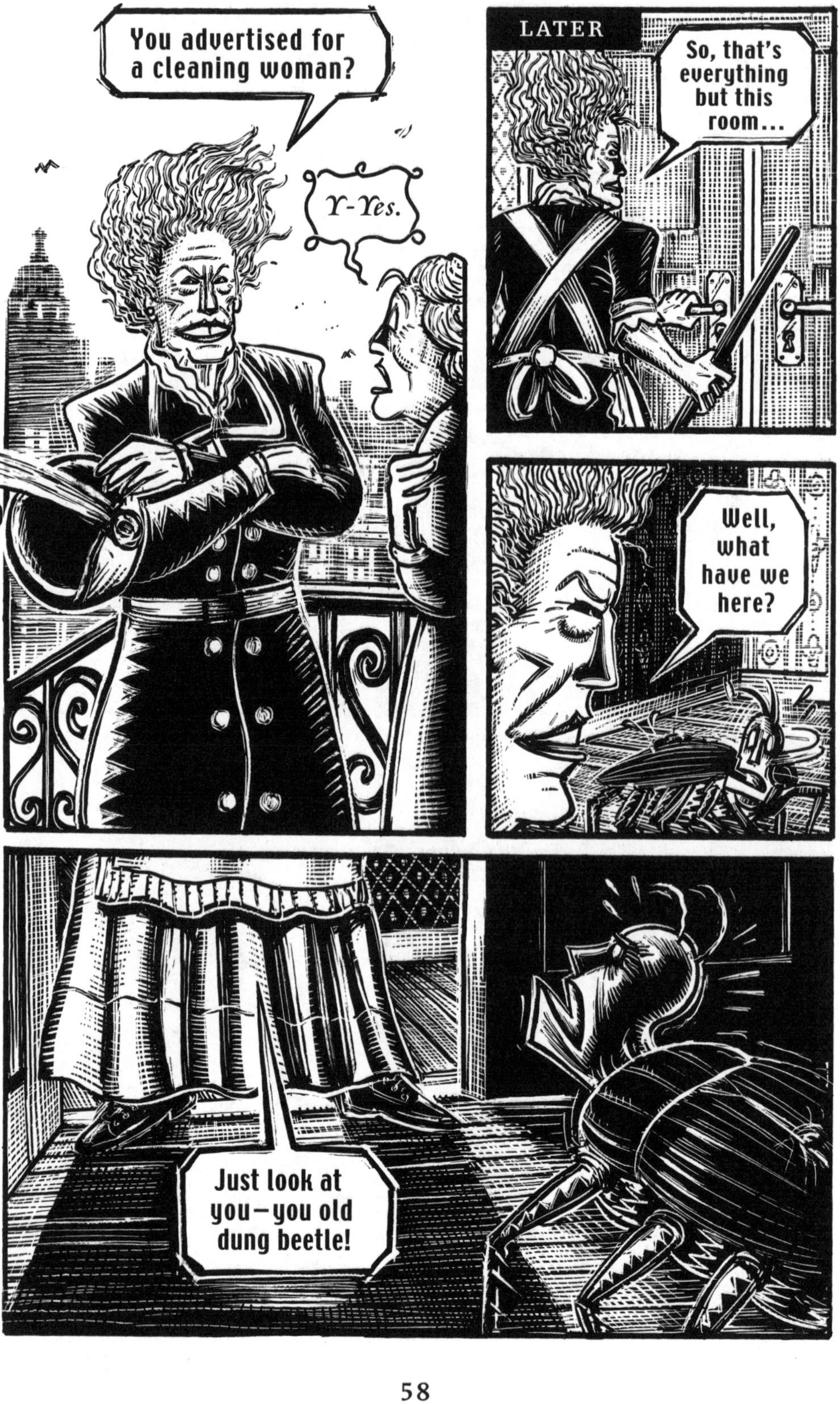
You advertised for a cleaning woman?
Y-Yes.
LATER
So, that's everything but this room...
Well, what have we here?
Just look at you—you old dung beetle!

62

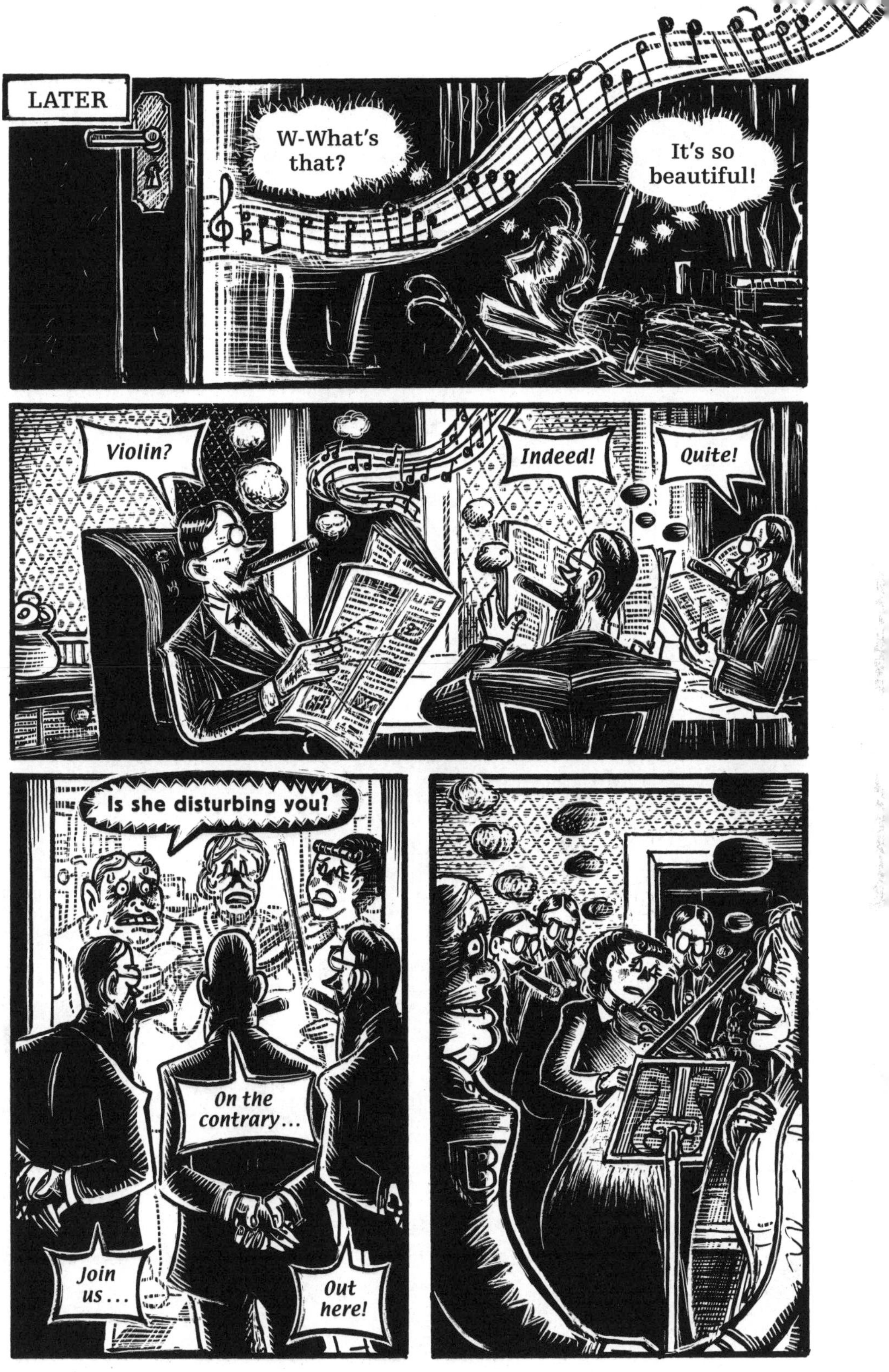
LATER
W-What's that?
It's so beautiful!
Violin?
Indeed!
Quite!
Is she disturbing you?
On the contrary...
Join us...
Out here!

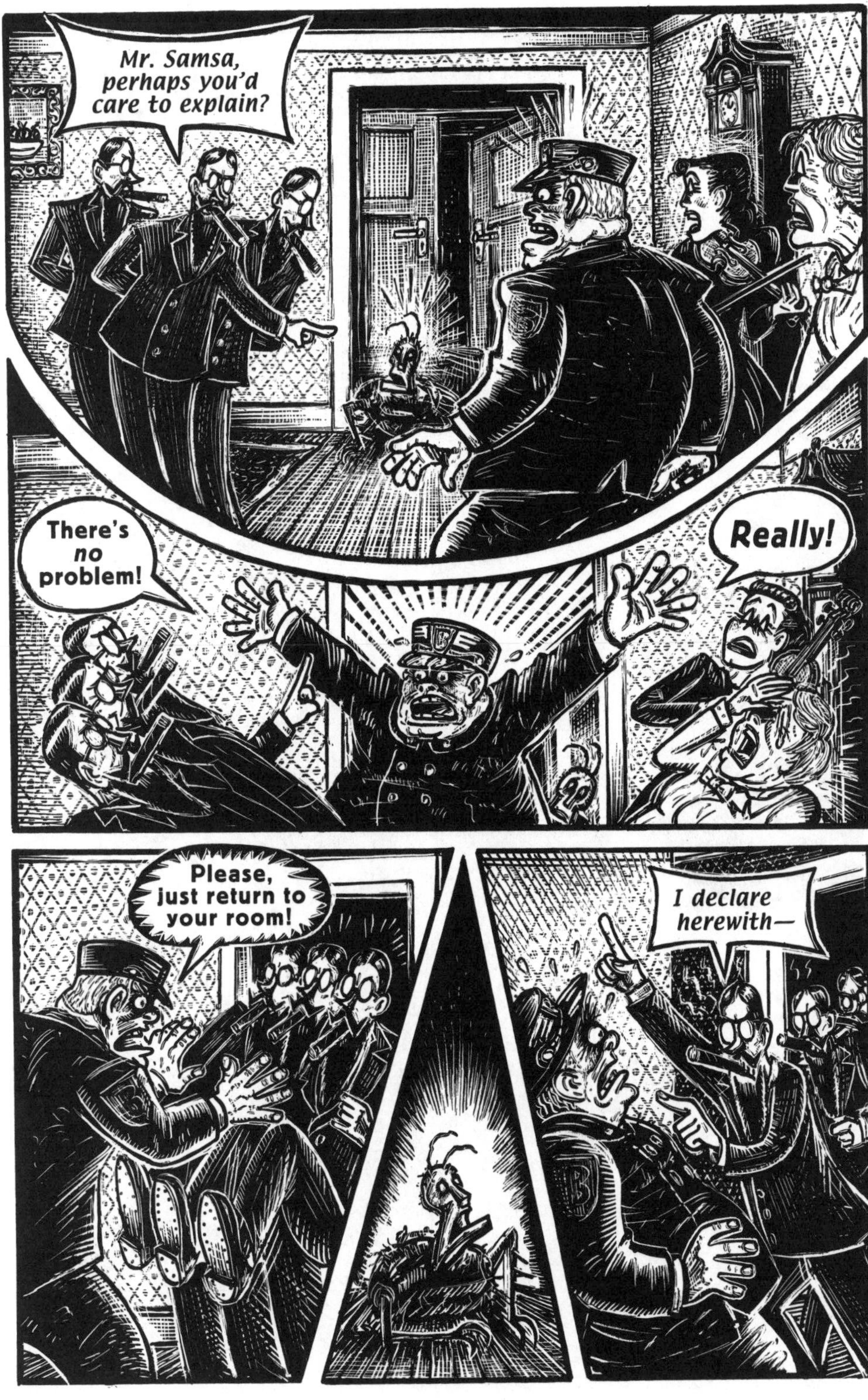

Mr. Samsa, perhaps you'd care to explain?
There's *no* problem!
Really!
Please, just return to your room!
I declare herewith—

66

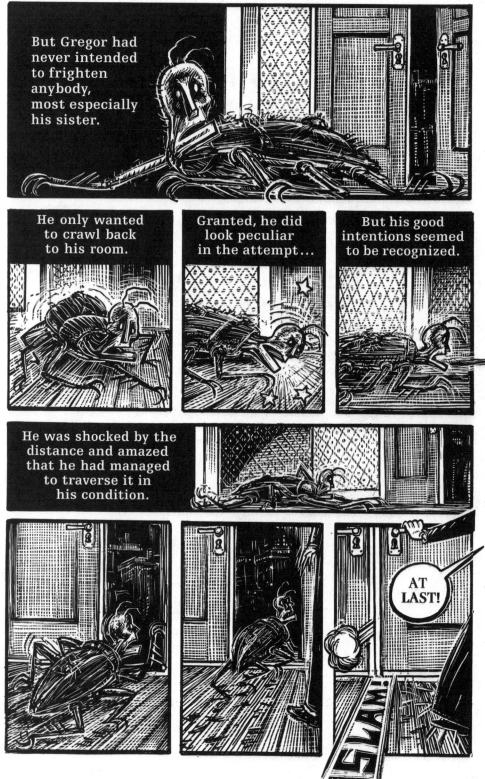

But Gregor had never intended to frighten anybody, most especially his sister.

He only wanted to crawl back to his room.

Granted, he did look peculiar in the attempt...

But his good intentions seemed to be recognized.

He was shocked by the distance and amazed that he had managed to traverse it in his condition.

AT LAST!

SLAM!

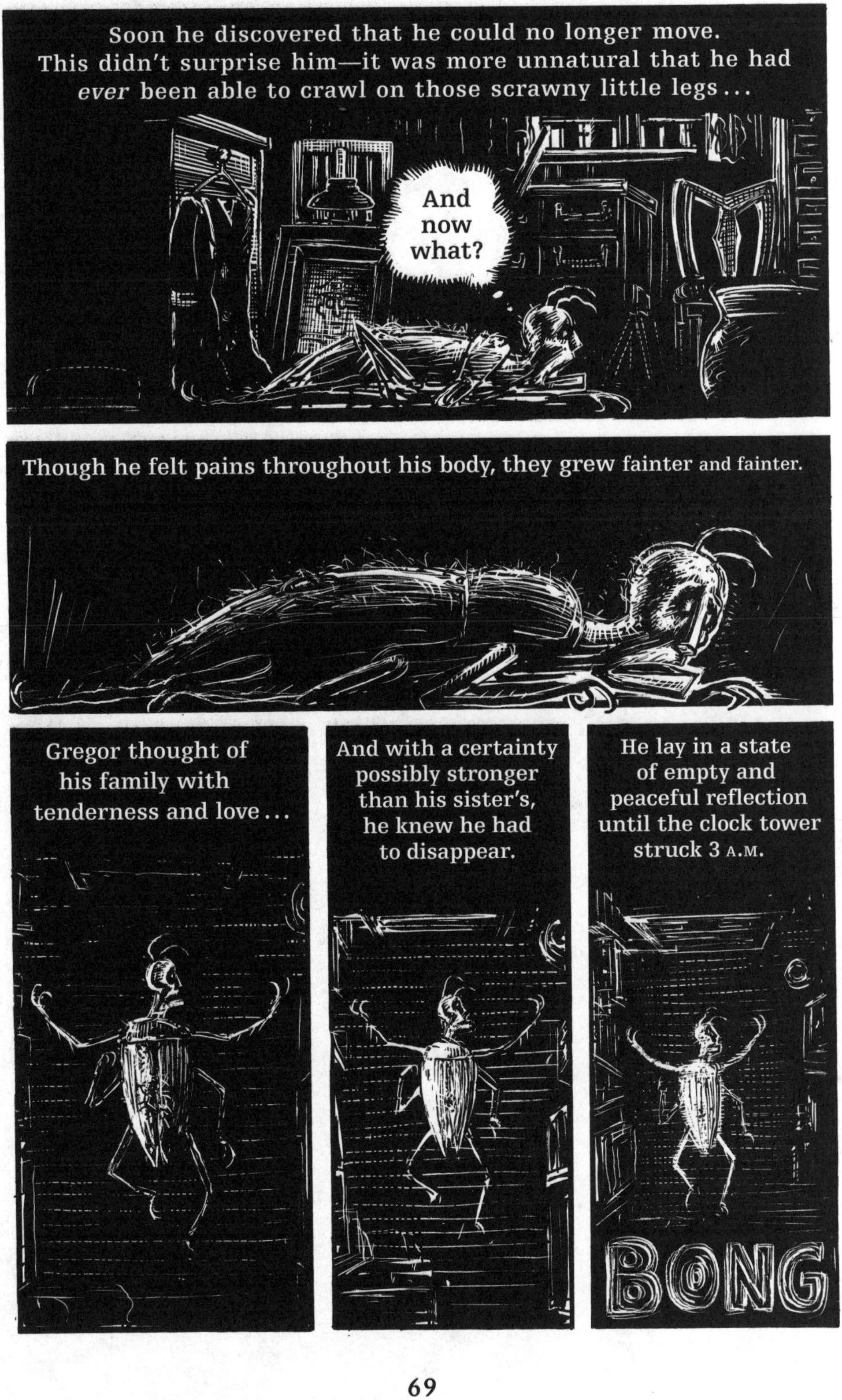
Soon he discovered that he could no longer move.
This didn't surprise him—it was more unnatural that he had *ever* been able to crawl on those scrawny little legs...
And now what?
Though he felt pains throughout his body, they grew fainter and fainter.
Gregor thought of his family with tenderness and love...
And with a certainty possibly stronger than his sister's, he knew he had to disappear.
He lay in a state of empty and peaceful reflection until the clock tower struck 3 A.M.
BONG

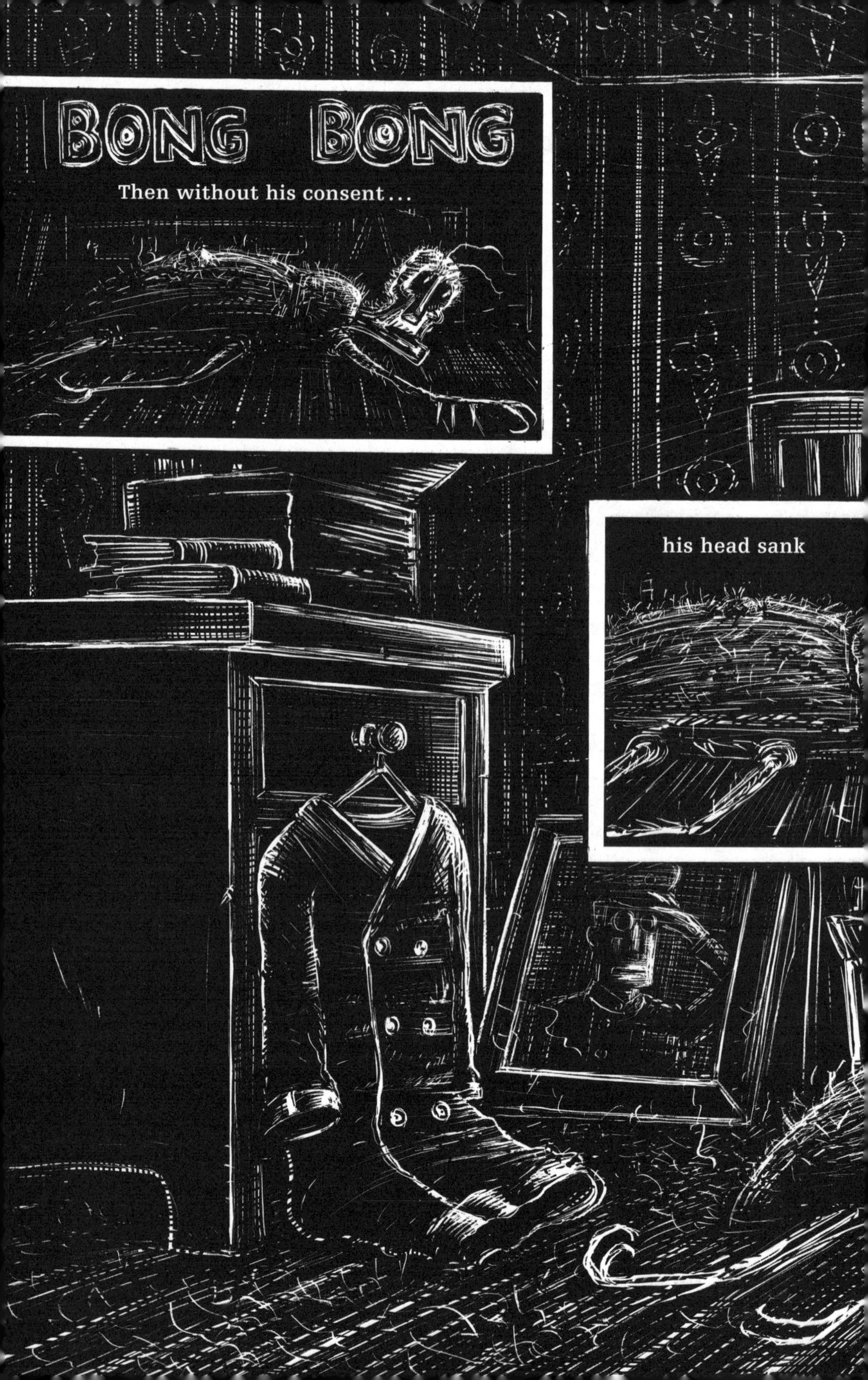
BONG BONG
Then without his consent...
his head sank

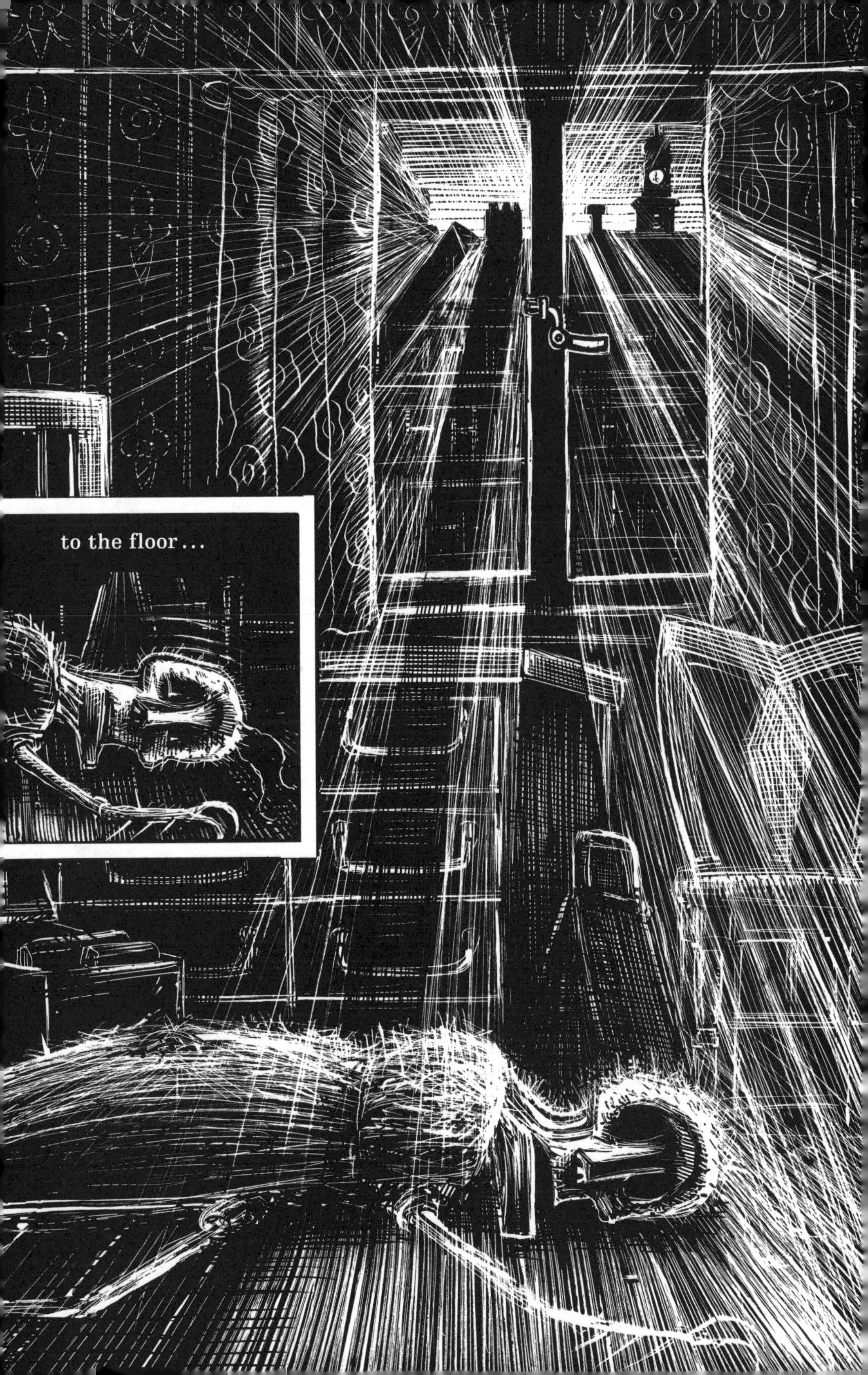
to the floor . . .

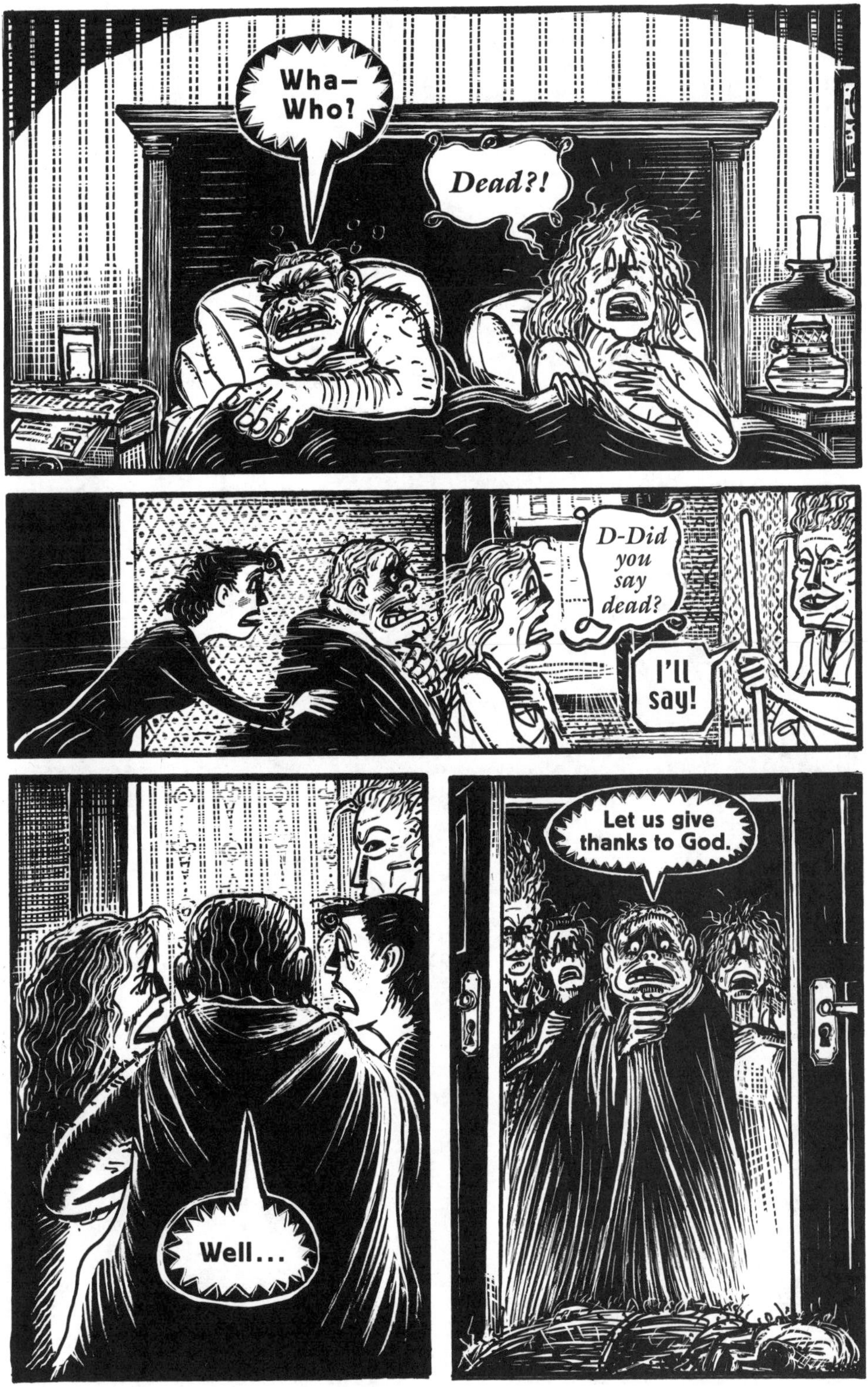
Wha–
Who?
Dead?!
D-Did you say dead?
I'll say!
Well...
Let us give thanks to God.

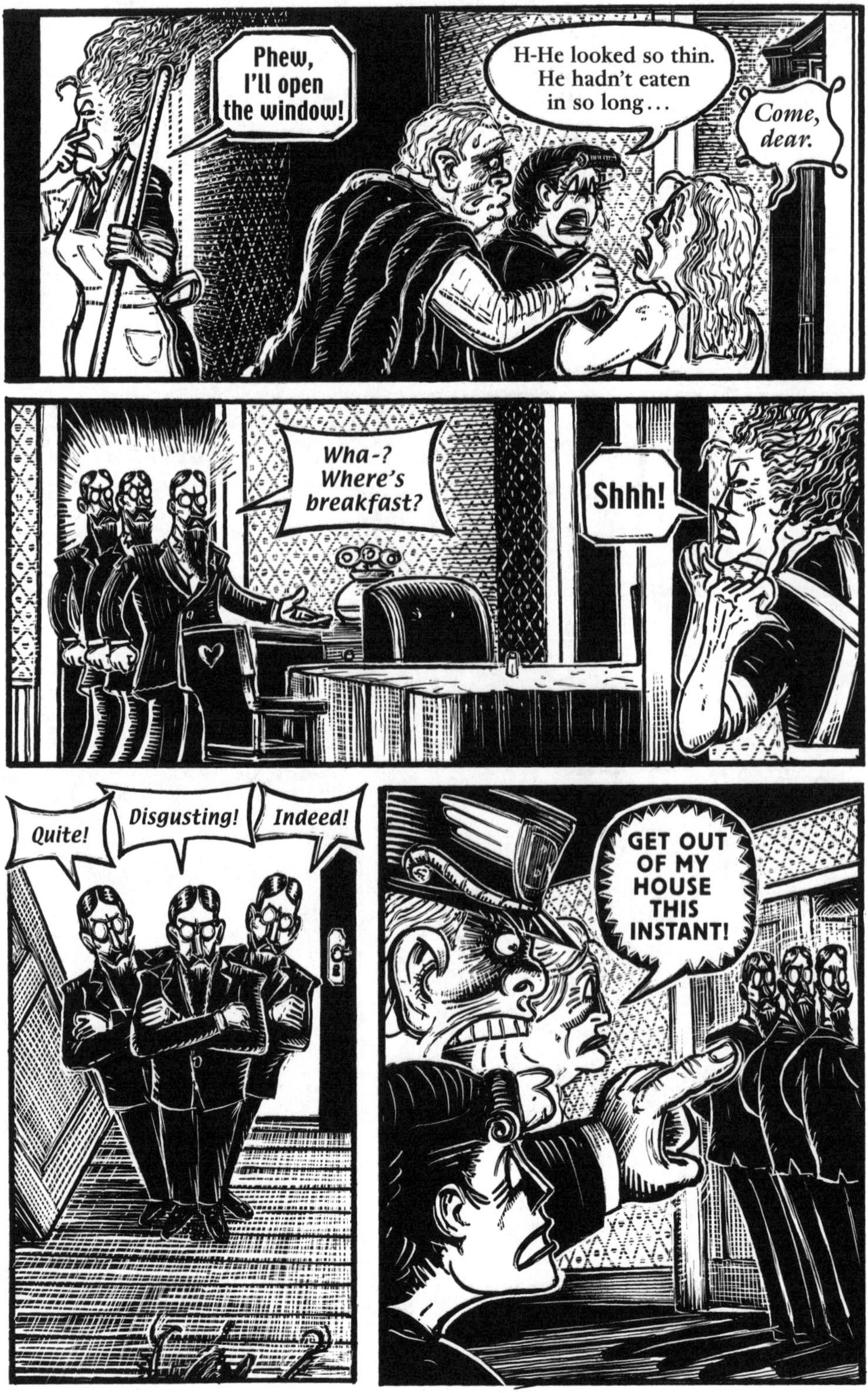
Phew, I'll open the window!
H-He looked so thin. He hadn't eaten in so long...
Come, dear.
Wha-? Where's breakfast?
Shhh!
Quite!
Disgusting!
Indeed!
GET OUT OF MY HOUSE THIS INSTANT!

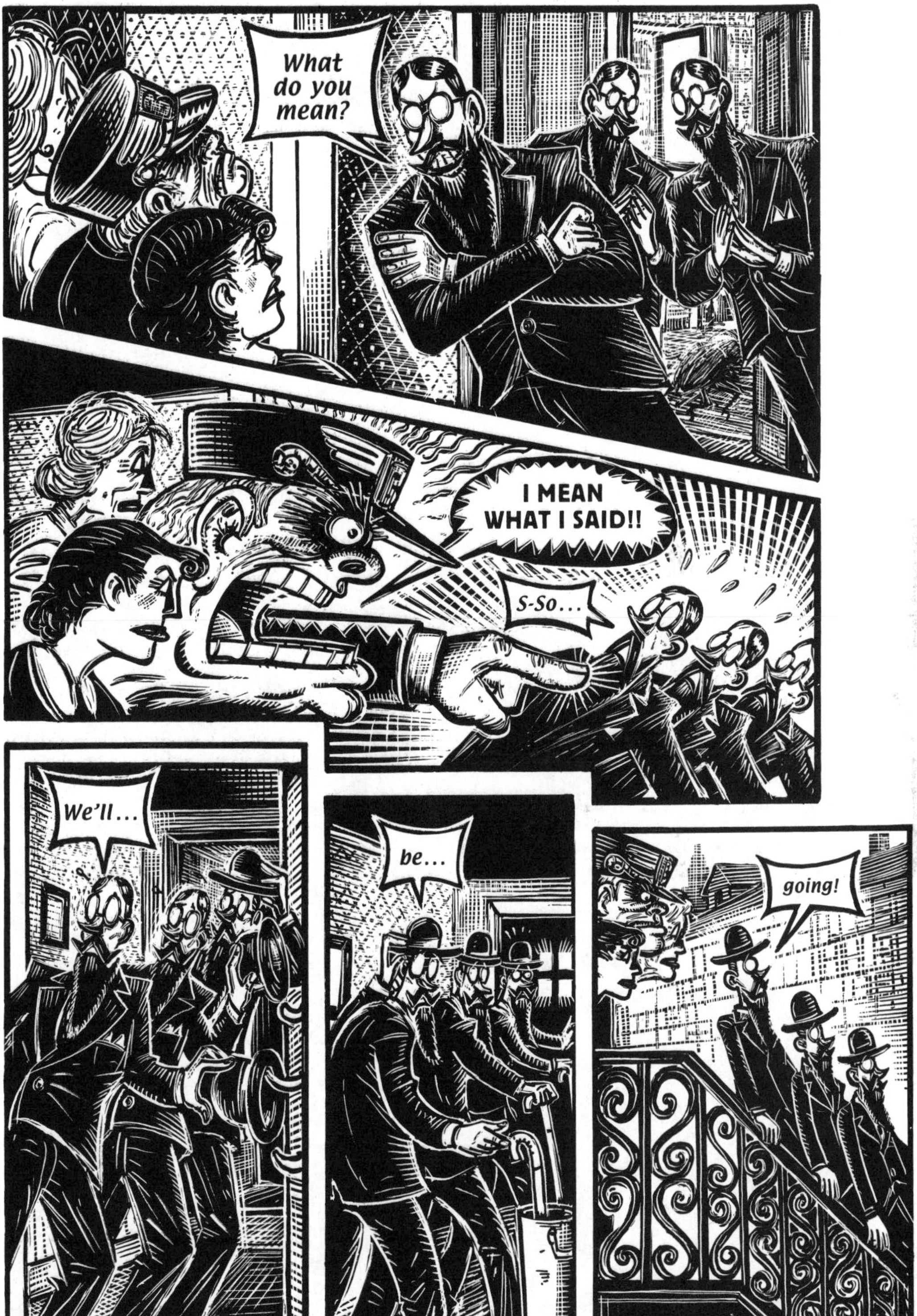
What do you mean?
I MEAN WHAT I SAID!!
S-So...
We'll...
be...
going!

...then we'll move to a better-situated apartment and...
Almost simultaneously it dawned on Mr. and Mrs. Samsa that, in spite of all the recent sorrows, Grete had blossomed into a beautiful and voluptuous girl...

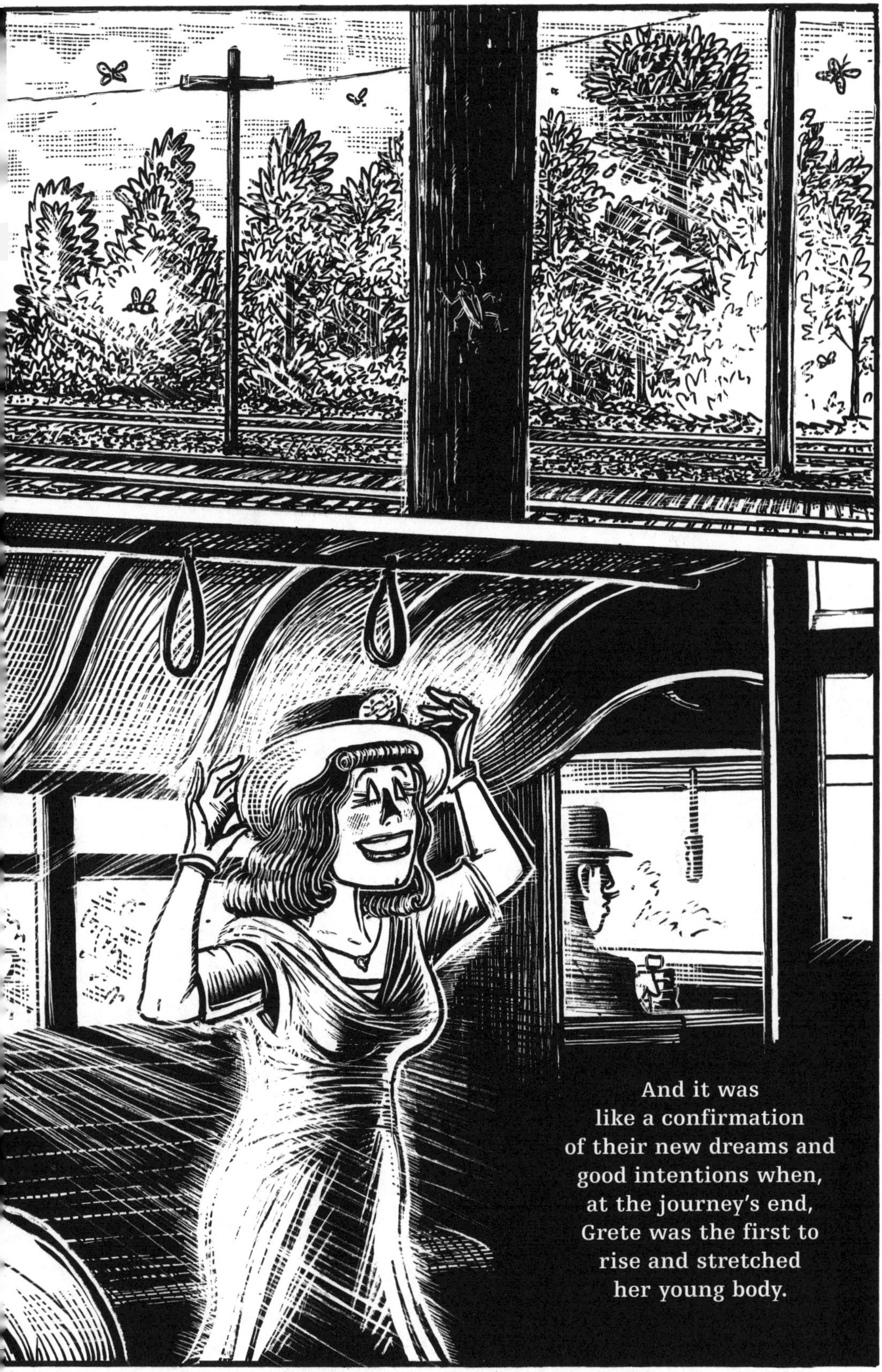
And it was like a confirmation of their new dreams and good intentions when, at the journey's end, Grete was the first to rise and stretched her young body.

ACKNOWLEDGMENTS

Thanks and appreciation to a great number of people who helped bring this project to light:

my beautiful wife, **BETTY RUSSELL**, for all her marvelous suggestions and eternal patience; **STEVE ROSS**, my longtime friend, and **CHRIS JACKSON**, my diligent editor, at Crown; **TERRY NANTIER** at NBM for years of support; **RYAN INZANA** for his endless assistance; **JOHN THOMAS** for lending his legal expertise; **EMILY RUSSELL** for her fantastic editorial eye; **KERSTIN HASENPUSCH** for a fine job of translating; **SUSY BERNSTEIN** for her scholarly perspective; **GAHAN WILSON**, **WILL EISNER**, and **JULES FEIFFER** for their ongoing encouragement; **MY EVER SUPPORTIVE FAMILY**; my friends **TONY**, **MOLLY**, **PHILIP**, **SCOTT**, **ELENA**, and **SETH**; and especially my daughter, **EMILY**, for "bug book" enthusiasms. Finally, thanks to **FRANZ KAFKA**, who was kind enough to put pen to paper in the first place and create a masterpiece.

STOP FORGETTING
TO
REMEMBER
STOP
FORGETTING
THE AUTOBIOGRAPHY OF WALTER KURTZ
TO
REMEMBER
PETER KUPER

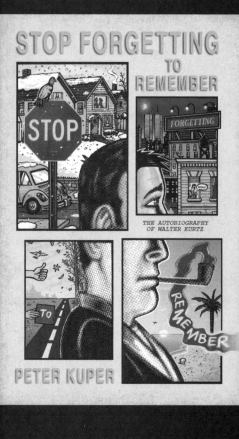